THE AUTHOR: Sheila Bir
contemporary writers on
the county makes her the i
schoolteacher, she is now
specialising in Cornwall an

THE AUTHOR Sheila Bird is amongst the best known of contemporary writers on Cornwall, and her knowledge of the county makes her the ideal guide to its villages. A former schoolteacher, she is now a full time writer and journalist, specialising in Cornwall and the West Country

The Book of Cornish Villages

Sheila Bird

Line drawings by Steve Hicks

DOVECOTE PRESS

To my father

First published in 1988 by The Dovecote Press Ltd
Stanbridge, Wimborne, Dorset BH21 4JD

ISBN 0 946159 51 3

Photoset by Character Graphics, Taunton, Somerset
Printed and bound by Biddles Ltd, Guildford and King's Lynn

Illustrations

Introduction

The Celtic land west of the Tamar, almost surrounded by water, has an identity very much its own. Within that land, bordered by a rugged coastline of spectacular cliffs, long, sweeping beaches, sandy coves and pleasing, work-a-day harbours, are the contrasting areas of desolate moorland, fertile farmland, deep, incised estuaries and wooded valleys. This is a landscape which gave rise not only to 'copper, fish and tin,' but also to the china clay, quarrying and agricultural industries, and increasingly to tourism, which now plays a vital role in the county's economy. This is a landscape from which legends, folklore and ghostly stories seem to spring spontaneously. This is a landscape inhabited by a proud people, who have an identity very much their own. For prior to the coming of the railways, Cornish folk had remained somewhat isolated from mainstream Britain. In earlier times, when trade and communication was mostly by water, they had closer associations with their Celtic cousins in Wales, in Ireland and especially in Brittany.

It is said, somewhat romantically perhaps, that the Phoenicians came to Cornwall in quest of tin, and, more substantially, that oyster dredging was carried out in the Fal and Helford rivers in Roman times. Settlements grew up around the fishing coves, waterways, mining areas and along the early routes into Cornwall. By virtue of its situation, close to the Western Approaches, Cornwall has long played an important role in Britain's defence and communications systems. A series of fortifications was constructed along the coast, some ports became naval dockyards in times of war and fighter stations were established in strategic sites during the Second World War. Thus prestige and prosperity emerged in Cornwall in a variety of ways, adding new dimensions to life around the county.

For Cornish villagers, everyday life was a struggle, but they have long demonstrated their resourcefulness and strength of character. The villages were self sufficient and most families remained in the locality of their birth. Few people worked far from the village; they knew each other and everybody knew what everybody else was doing, which was a stabilising influence for the would-be wayward. Life revolved around the church or chapel, with the local inn, shops and school cementing the community. High days and holidays were anticipated with pleasure and savoured in restrospect. Each village had its saint and feasten day, when every family, however poor, endeavoured to celebrate with a special roast meat and figgy pudden, along with such delights as current and saffron cakes, or 'heavy' cake, eaten hot with lashings of clotted cream, rather than the usual basic fare, which tended to be scraps of almost anything baked in a pie. Indeed, rumour had it that the Devil himself, having crossed the Tamar, reflected on there being more saints in Cornwall than there were in heaven, and fearing that he might end up in a pie, turned smartly and rapidly retreated.

The status of towns, villages and hamlets fluctuates from time to time, with former boroughs declining and some villages gaining in importance. In selecting the places to be included I have chosen many old favourites, but have made a particular point of seeking out little known places which have an interesting story to tell. In Cornwall a 'church town' is not a town, it refers to the area around the old parish church, a 'town place' can be a farmyard, while a number of the villages are considerably bigger than some towns. Similarly, the county of Cornwall should not be confused with the Duchy, for that is a term given to the Duke of Cornwall's estates here and elsewhere, and they do not encompass the whole of the county. They were founded in 1336 from the Norman earldom to create revenue for the heir to the throne.

In this gazeteer the places are related to their context in the landscape, while themes such as the development of canals and railways, engineering, quarrying, mining, fishing, ships, shipwrecks, lifeboats, smuggling, personalities, legends, folklore, witchcraft, ghosts, superstitions, writers and artists run through the book. It might be helpful to point out that 'bal' and 'wheal' mean mine, a small pilchard is a sardine, and a weathered formation of saucer shaped rocks, where bigger stones pivot on smaller, is known as a cheesewring. *Fogou* = a prehistoric cavern, *quoit* = chamber tomb, *cromlech* = Neolithic chieftain's burial chamber, *dinas* = hill fort, *mên* or *maen* = stone, *carn* = heap of stones, *pen* = headland, *pol* = pool, *port* = cove, *enys* = island, *praze* = common, *towan* = sandhill, while *tre* denotes a dwelling place.

My thanks go to Terry Knight of the Local Studies Library, Redruth, for all his painstaking help and advice, librarians and the folk around the villages who have helped me in my researches over many years. Thanks also to Duncan Warren, David Clarke, Ralph Bird, Austin Wormleighton, and to Stephen Hicks for his delightful illustrations.

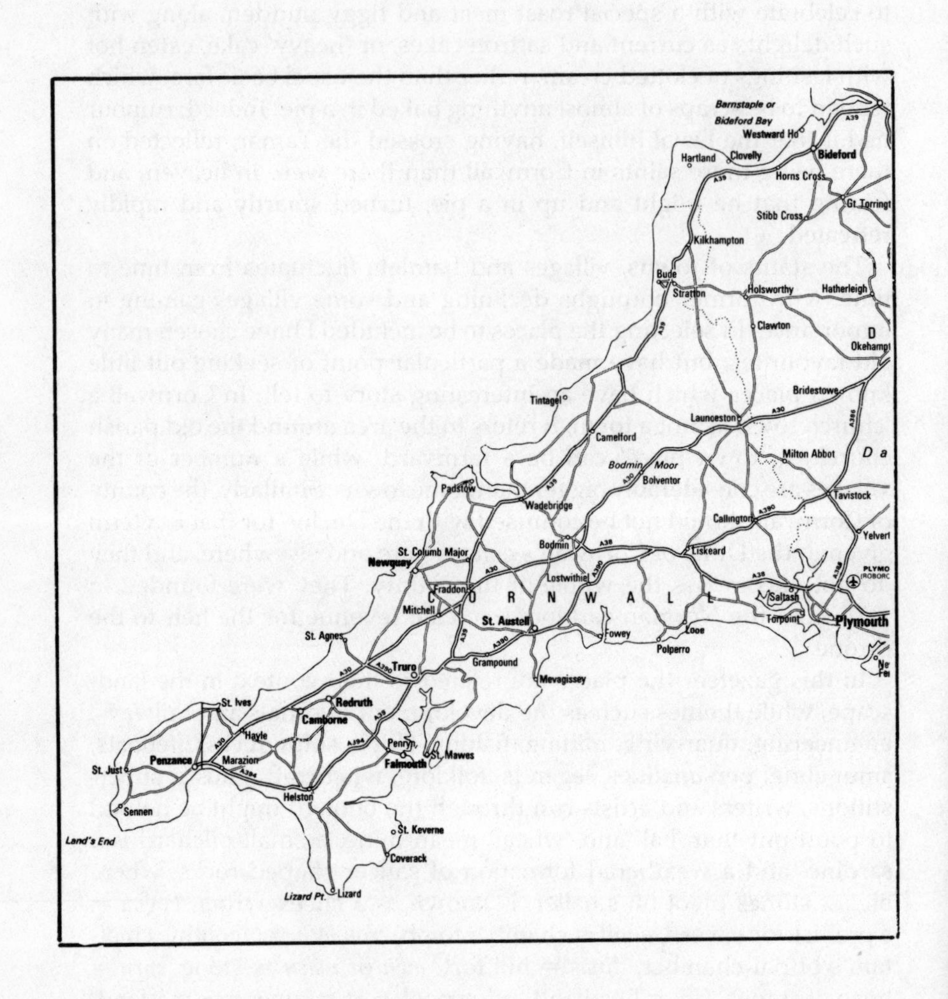

Barnstaple or
Bideford Bay
Westward Ho
Bideford
Hartland
Clovelly
Horns Cross
Stibb Cross
Kilkhampton
Bude
Stratton
Holsworthy
Hatherleigh
Clawton
Bridestowe
Tintagel
Launceston
Camelford
Milton Abbot
Bodmin Moor
Bolventor
Padstow
Tavistock
Wadebridge
Callington
Bodmin
Liskeard
St. Columb Major
Newquay
Lostwithiel
Fraddon
C O R N W A L L
Saltash
Mitchell
Torpoint
Plymouth
St. Austell
Fowey
Looe
St. Agnes
Polperro
Grampound
Truro
Mevagissey
St. Ives
Redruth
Camborne
Hayle
Penryn
Falmouth
St. Mawes
St. Just
Penzance
Marazion
Helston
Sennen
St. Keverne
Land's End
Coverack
Lizard Pt.
Lizard
A39
A30
A386
A38
A390
A394

Advent *see* St. Breward

Alternun

Streams rising in the peaty areas of West Moor, to the north of Bolventor, flow as Penpont Water beneath the bridges of Alternun, before combining with the Inny and Tamar rivers. Attractive cottages line the village street at Alternun (the Altar of St Nonna), and its church, often referred to as 'the cathedral of the moor' has a tall, pinnacled tower constructed from surface granite found on Bodmin Moor. In early spring snowdrops add to its charm, whilst the famous well was reputed to have powers of curing insanity. An early brand of 'shock' tactics was employed here, for unfortunate patients were violently thrust in and out of the water until all traces of insanity disappeared. If a cure was effected, prayers were offered to the saint, otherwise the treatment continued.

A relief effigy of John Wesley above the door of the former chapel was fashioned by Nevill Northey Burnard, a stonemason's son born in 1818, who displayed a natural gift for stone carving as a boy, when he used a nail as an improvised tool. At the age of 15 he went to work for Squire Treffry at Fowey, later becoming one of the country's top sculptors. But drink was to be his downfall. Returning to Cornwall in tragic circumstances, he took to the road, died penniless in Redruth workhouse, and was buried in a pauper's grave in Camborne.

John Wesley stayed with Elizabeth and Digory Isbell at nearby Trewint, where Wesley's Cottage remains as a memorial to him, and where an annual service is held on 24th May.

A network of secondary lanes through refreshingly unspoilt countryside to the north, crosses the young river Inny, and leads to the villages of Laneast and St Clether, which both have holy wells. John Couch Adams, the astronomer and discoverer of the planet Neptune was born in the parish of Laneast. The old seat of the Trelawny family lies between Alternun and Laneast (see Pelynt). A farmhouse at Trerithick, two miles to the east, dated 1585, was originally built to an E shaped design.

Eastwards down the Inny lies Polyphant, which has long been famous for its beautiful, dove grey hornblende picrite, used in many Cornish churches and in the building of Launceston Castle. It was also useful in the manufacture of candles, inkstands and functional ornaments, as well as for decorative stonework.

Angarrack

Angarrack is particularly interesting for its early industrial and transport links. In 1801 there had been an abortive scheme to link the mining areas with the port of Hayle by means of a canal from Carwinn Bridge via Angarrack. Following the success of the *Redruth and Chacewater* mineral railway, which opened in 1826, a company was formed to construct a railway from Hayle to Tresavean to serve the numerous mines around Redruth and Camborne. An intended branch from Angarrack to Helston would have catered for the Godolphin and Breage mining areas, but the plan was abandoned. Initially the steep incline at Angarrack was worked by a stationary engine and wire rope, with the western section worked by horses. In 1843, improved brake power allowed engines to negotiate the incline with trucks. At that time it was a source of satisfaction to the company that their technology was ahead of the *Redruth and Chacewater Railway*, which was still relying on horse traction.

With the opening up of rail passenger routes in 1841, bringing more travellers to the South West, a regular service was introduced. Stations were set up between Hayle and Redruth, including one at Angarrack. The inauguration provided a good excuse for the usual celebrations, including free rail travel for all. On this historic occasion, the engine was put out of gear at the top off the incline, the carriages were made fast to a wire rope attached to the stationary engine, and lowered slowly, at less than walking pace. Although well controlled, it tested the nerves of some of the passengers, who must have heaved sighs of relief on reaching the bottom. Then the engine was restarted and they chugged on to Copperhouse, changing to horse traction to complete the trip to Hayle Foundry.

Antony House

When the new Hayle branchline linking with Penzance, opened in 1852, much of the line, including the Angarrack incline was abandoned. The original timber viaduct, 266 yards long and a 100 feet high replaced the steep incline. This in turn was replaced by the stone viaduct constructed between 1881 and 1885. There were several fatalities during its building. The men involved in bridge construction were skilled, took a great pride in their work, and were much respected. Angarrack station closed on 16th February 1852.

Antony

Antony, on the estuary of the River Lynher, just to the west of Torpoint, was an established seat of the Carew family from the 15th century, as memorials in the church of St James testify. Also in the church is a canopied brass to Margery Arundell (1420), considered to be the most spectacular early brass in Cornwall. Further to the historical theme, the cannon balls outside Antony House were fired in anger during Charles I's siege of Plymouth during the 17th century.

Richard Carew, a remarkable scholar and man of many parts was born at the old house in 1555, went up to Christ Church, Oxford, at the age of eleven and then on to Clements Inn. But he returned to Cornwall to run the family estates, and devoted every spare moment to learning, teaching himself Greek, Dutch, Spanish, French and Italian as well as becoming an author and poet. His *Survey of Cornwall*, written between 1585 and 1594 offers a social, architectural and topographical insight into Elizabethan Cornwall. He also became a Justice and Sheriff of Cornwall, commanding the troops defending the Tamar estuary against possible invasion at the time of the Armada. A great fisherman, he created a saltwater fishpool on the shores of the river, where he used to tap a stone with his walking stick to summon the fish to come and be fed.

Richard Carew's grandsons were to divide the family loyalties at the time of the Civil War. The elder became governor of St Nicholas (now Drake's) Island in Plymouth Sound, changed his allegiance and was beheaded, while his Parliamentarian younger brother also lost his head for his beliefs.

Antony House, built in 1721 of silver grey Pentewan stone, and described by John Betjeman as being 'far the most distinguished classic country house of its date in Cornwall', came into the possession of the National Trust in 1961. Nearby Antony Wood has been leased to the Woodland Trust by Sir John Carew for the conservation of specialist woodland.

It is rumoured that the Devil once crossed into Cornwall on nearby Torpoint ferry, but reflecting that the Cornish had a penchant for creating saints or sticking almost anything in a pie and baking it, he hurriedly retreated.

Ashton, *see* St Dominick

Blisland

The picturesque village of Blisland, on the western slopes of Bodmin Moor, situated where a network of narrow lanes converge, is grouped around a Saxon style village green, rarely found in Cornwall. To the south of the green is the Norman church, dedicated to St Protus and St Hyacinth; its bright interior and design much appreciated by John Betjeman, who wrote of the village, 'Its glory is its church.' John Kempe's monument of 1728 assures us, 'Here's Peace and Rest.'

In May 1895 the church was the setting for a strange act of penance, which turned into an unholy farce. Two village lads had taken advantage of a local lass. Given the option of prosecution or making public confessions in church, they opted for the latter; a decision which attracted an unusually large and enthusiastic congregation, with standing room only. After being sternly admonished, they were led by the rector to the churchyard gates, carrying loaves of bread under their arms, to be distributed to the congregation as an act of atonement. But the intended symbolism was lost as the congregation pushed and shoved in an effort to grab the loaves, and when an irreverent lad passed around an enormous tin of treacle the whole thing turned into a sticky, exuberant jamboree, which thereafter became known as 'Bread and Treacle Sunday.'

Architecturally interesting are the old, gabled manor house, which puzzles the experts by having Norman windows and a Norman arch, and nearby Lavethan, constructed in 1653, but incorporating 15th century work. This also is an area of interesting bridges. At Bradford, to the north, there are clapper bridges across the De Lank river, reckoned to be amongst the best in Cornwall, while to the north west is Poley's bridge across the River Camel, constructed in 1848, with five arches built with huge granite slabs.

The surrounding area is rich in pre-history, with stone circles, hut circles and Stripple Stones. Henge Monument on Hawkstor Downs has a circular bank and an internal ditch, enclosing an irregular ring of 15 stones. Jubilee Rock on Pendrift Common is a massive granite boulder, bearing carvings by John Rogers, to commemorate George III's jubilee.

Bolventor

Bolventor, a tiny hamlet just off the Bodmin to Launceston road has a little granite church with a central bellcote, a handful of cottages and a school catering for children from the outlying farms and small-holdings. But for generations of travellers the name 'Bolventor' recalls the romantic Jamaica Inn, originally an 18th century coaching inn, serving needs of passengers and horses, which became immortalised in Daphne du Maurier's novel. It is now slate hung, with gables and windows in the Tudor style. The ghost of a murdered sailor reputedly returned here from time to time to finish his drink. Although associated with smuggling and colourful fiction, the area is impressive in its natural wild beauty, becoming melancholic and brooding beneath a heavy skyscape, and isolated and atmospheric as the moorland mists roll in.

A mile to the south east of Bolventor is Dozmary Pool, a vast lonely expanse of water, about a mile in circumference. This is sometimes claimed to be the lake into which Sir Bedivere thrust King Arthur's sword Excalibur. Folklore surrounding Tregeagle, who reputedly sold

Jamaica Inn, Bolventor

his soul to the Devil, recounted that amongst his penances was the seemingly impossible task of emptying Dozmary Pool with a leaky limpet shell. This, and the myth about Dozmary Pool being bottomless were exploded in the last century, when the pool actually dried out, but connoisseurs of colourful stories tend to discount such details.

In the late 1870s, James Henderson of Truro set up an ice manufacturing depot at Dozmary Pool, described in *The West Briton* as being, 'one of the most dismal spots in Cornwall.' It was said that one acre of frozen water a foot thick would produce a thousand tons of ice, and that seven tons of ice per day could be compressed here. It was distributed by rail to fish buyers in Cornwall and London. In December 1877, a hurricane ripped off the roof of one of the ice houses, depositing it some distance across Bodmin Moor.

The painters Harold and Laura Knight found this an inspirational place, and stayed in a hut overlooking the pool.

Brown Gelly, to the south of the pool and rising to about a thousand feet above sea level, is surrounded by cairns, barrows and hut circles. To the north of the A30, Brown Willy at 1,375 feet above sea level is the highest point in Cornwall. On Rough Tor (1312ft) is a small hill fort with hut circles.

Boscastle

The village of Boscastle, with its old world charm, and delightful little harbour lying at the foot of its steep main street, featured as Castle Boterel in Thomas Hardy's *A Pair of Blue Eyes*, published in 1873. Its attractive and unusual name stemmed from Botreaux Castle, which has long since disappeared. The Valency and Jordan rivers rush down steep sided combes to the ancient, picturesque and almost landlocked harbour, with its two stone jetties. The outer arm was damaged when a floating mine exploded in the last war, and granite from Plymouth's old Laira Bridge was used in its repair. In certain conditions the blow hole in the harbour can propel a spectacular jet across its entrance, with loud and impressive accoustics.

Old Boscastle possessed many inns. The cleric and poet Robert Stephen Hawker, who visited the Ship Inn with a friend in the last century, was bemused by the hospitality offered by the eccentric landlady. This was somewhat surprising in view of the fact that he was a noted eccentric himself (see Morwenstow). In response to their request for beds for the night, they were given to understand that more sophisticated travellers usually slept two in a bed. Enquiries about what was on the menu drew the response, 'meat and taties';

the meat they later discovered to have been roast seal.

The shipping trade at Boscastle picked up when vast quantities of iron ore were brought here from Trebursye (near Launceston) by steam engines pulling trucks along the road. They returned carrying imported coal for the mines. The first locomotive completed the journey in April 1862, but the project was fraught with difficulties, and repair work was continually being carried out. Locals blamed the engines for horses bolting and the sparks that set fire to a man's shirt as he innocently toiled in a field.

Boscastle has no church. Its mother church is at Minster, but Forrabury church, in an exposed situation on a hill to the south is nearer. Dating from Norman times, this has a short, plain west tower. An intriguing explanation for the silent church tower was that when a fine peal of bells was being brought in by sea, the pilot thanked God for a safe voyage. This displeased the skipper who reckoned that God might be thanked on land, but a skipper and his ship should get the credit at sea. Then a sudden tempest engulfed the ship, sending all to their doom, apart from the God-fearing pilot, who reached these shores safely. Some say that violent storms can set the ghostly bells a-ringing. The artist J. M. W. Turner caught the essence of this striking seascape in a painting from Willapark Point.

Nearby Trevalga has a church dating from Norman times, with an ancient cross near the porch. A holed rock on the cliff goes by the name of the Ladies' Window, with Short Island just off-shore.

Bossiney

The village of Bossiney grew up around the old castle, which is now grass-covered and known as Bossiney Mound. The settlement originally depended on fishing, and was united with Trevena (Tintagel) to become a borough, sending two members to Parliament. A one-time representative was Sir Francis Drake. However, the borough declined in importance during the 16th century. According to Arthurian legend, the Round Table of King Arthur lies beneath the mound, and rises briefly in a flash of silver light on Midsummer Eve.

Rocky Valley is noted for its scenery, with tumbling waters, leafiness, rocks, ferns and wild flowers, and was once the haunt of the Cornish chough. Well marked footpaths lead to St Nectan's Kieve, where the water descends into the basin (kieve), before cascading in waterfalls, to charming effect. St Nectan, brother to Morwenna of Morwenstow, occupied a hermitage above the pool, and died at Hartland, where the church is dedicated to him.

Botallack

This old mining village near St Just on the extreme west coast inspired the story *Deep Down*, by R. M. Ballantyne, who visited the area in 1868. The mines also had an effect on Wilkie Collins, who visited them while on holiday in the summer of 1851, and reflected the experience in his writings. Twelve year old Prince Arthur descended the diagonal mineshaft at Botallack in 1862, and Lady Falmouth and her daughter visited the mine just a week before an appalling accident in April 1863, when a skip hurtled out of control to the bottom of the shaft, killing eleven people.

Carn Kenidjack, about a mile to the east, is also referred to as the 'Hooting Carn', on account of the eerie noises issuing forth of a dark night, when mysterious shapes and strange lights dart around, and a phantom cloaked horseman gallops silently amid the stone relics. It is said that two miners who strayed here after drinking at Morvah accepted the horseman's invitation to watch the giants wrestling up on the Carn. When one contestant fell to the ground, apparently dead the two men rushed forward to comfort him; only to be whisked away by a whirlwind and deposited, tired and frightened in the midst of the moor.

On a headland to the west is Kenidjack Castle, an Iron Age fort with a double rampart. Cape Cornwall, lying just to the south has the distinction of being the only headland designated a 'Cape' in England and Wales. The Brisons, a group of rocks to the south west have borne grim witness to many a shipwreck, while the area to the east is rich in archaeological interest.

Botus Fleming

The village lies in a sheltered valley near the Tamar estuary, where the traditional apple and cherry orchards made it a particular delight in spring. A twelve foot high obelisk in a field recalls William Martyn, a Christian who died in 1762 requesting to be buried in unconsecrated ground, for he had 'no superstitious veneration for church or churchyard'.

Inside the church of St Mary is a stone figure of a knight, possibly representing the crusader Stephen de Fleming, who left his name to the village. North east, across the creek and on the banks of the Tamar, are the hamlets of Tinnell, Wayton, Clifton and Cargreen, amid pleasing marsh and estuary scenery. A ferry once lined Cargreen with Devon. Landulph's church of St Leonard bears witness to the area's former touch of eastern promise, for here lie the mortal remains of Theodore Palaeologus, a descendant of the medieval Christian Emperors of Byzantium, who died at Clifton in 1636. There is also a monument to Sir Nicholas Lower of Clifton (1655). In the churchyard is a granite sundial dated 1690. To the south of the village is Kingsmill Lake.

Breage

Breage, just over a mile inland from Mount's Bay lies in an area which saw an influx of Irish folk in the 6th century. A holed sandstone, rare in this area, was fabled to have been carved from granite stained red with the blood shed during this invasion.

The place abounds with colourful stories. The 15th century church is dedicated to St Breaca, the sister of St Euny. Tradition says that the parish, originally known as Penbro, was renamed in her honour because she helped provide the church bells. The tower supposedly housed the largest bells in Cornwall, but a former vicar who disliked their sound had them melted down to create one so heavy that it took three strong men to ring it. An old rhyme which gave us some idea what the men got up to when they were not ringing church bells ran thus:

'God keep us from rocks and shelving sands,
From Germoe men and Breage hands.'

Nicknames, mostly insulting, and describing physical characteristics or habits were traditional in Breage, where big families and the custom of handing down favourite names caused some confusion.

Breage miners prided themselves on being tougher than their counterparts from Poldice, who they reckoned stood up to their mine captains like mice, rather than men, for:

'Up Poldice the men are like mice,
And tin is good and plenty,
But Cap'n J. Teague, a man from Breage,
Will give 'ee ten for twenty.'

When mining was in recession in 1850, a company was formed in Breage to send men out to the Californian gold diggings; the first company of its kind in Cornwall. The adventurers were given a celebratory send-off at the Star Inn, before departing with their tents and tools. The stoppage of Wheal Vor, Great Work and other mines, together with the lessening off in the china clay and granite industries in the mid 1870s, resulted in empty houses and distressed families, with their breadwinners overseas. Derelict land was brought into cultivation in an effort to create more employment (see Gwennap).

Between here and Germoe is Tregonning Hill, rising to 635 feet, where William Cookworthy first realized the potential of china clay in 1746 (see St Stephen in Brannel). The Godophin family, who rose to prominence in the reign of Henry VIII, made their fortunes in the rich mining area around Godolphin Hill. Sidney Godolphin (1610-43), Queen Anne's Lord High Treasurer, and poet of promise was born here. He met an untimely death in the porchway of a Chagford inn, fighting for Charles I during the Civil War. The village of Godolphin Cross lies at the junction of secondary roads.

Bridges, *see* Luxulyan

Bugle, *see* Roche & Luxulyan

Cadgwith

Evocative old photographs of the picturesque fishing village on the Lizard peninsula, with its stone and thatch cottages, fishing boats, nets and pots, reflect its close affinity with Brittany. At the end of the last century, fishermen sat in contemplative fashion on the benches outside the white walled cottages, so intent on the water that they scarcely noticed the holiday makers who were just beginning to infiltrate the area. At the first sign of an approaching pilchard shoal, the dramatic cry of 'Hevva! Hevva!' resounded around the harbour, and intrigued newcomers stopped to watch the fishermen take to their boats.

It was an ill wind that made 1885 a good 'fish and taties' season here, for strong south westerlies prevented vessels rounding the Lizard and making for Newlyn, and catches were landed at Cadgwith instead. However, the pilchard industry gradually declined and in 1890 it was reported, 'Not a single pilchard has been caught by a seine on the Cornish coast.'

Traditionally the villagers' income had been supplemented by another age-old profession, for the old *Robbers' Retreat*, known colloquialy as the *Cadgwith Anthem* strongly urged:

'Come fill up your glasses and let us be merry,
For to rob bags of plunger, it is our intent.'

The young lads of Cadgwith followed their fathers as fishermen, as well as joining the navy, merchant service or becoming coastguards. Their seamanship later stood them in good stead for responsible positions as seiners, pilots or coxswains. The first lifeboat to come on station here in 1867 was the *Western Commercial Traveller*, and between then and the removal of the *Guide of Dunkirk* in 1963, 388 lives had been saved. The last lifeboat was renamed *Girl Guide* and became a fishing and pleasure boat, whilst Inshore Rescue Boats took over her role.

Amidst the surrounding caverns and intriguing rock formations is the *Devil's Frying Pan*, a collapsed cave which creates a blow hole when seas are rough.

Happily, Cadgwith still functions as a small fishing village, with the emphasis on crabs and lobsters.

Caerhayes, *see* **St Michael Caerhayes**

Calenick

Calenick, just south of Truro and situated at the head of a creek of the Truro River, was formerly an industrial place, with good access by water, and later by rail and road. Boats, ranging from small rowing boats to barges with a capacity of fifty tons, were constructed here. There were ropewalks, a candlemaking factory and an important smelting works.

Early in the last century it was customary to keep bees here, and the cottage gardens received the attentions of the light fingered (and tough skinned) gangs, who found it lucrative to work the Truro beat as part of the honey racket. Market gardeners supplied Truro with produce, and during the last war bee-keeping was again encouraged in the area.

The 18th century Calenick House bears traces of an older building. There is a slate-hung upper storey and a separate clock tower with cupula, dated 1752.

Cardinham

The pleasant village of Cardinham (meaning 'the town of the hillfort') lies on the edge of Bodmin Moor, to the east of Bodmin, in a landscape characterised by moorland and steep wooded valleys. A network of ancient trackways indicates its former importance. Bury Castle lies a mile to the north east, and Cardinham Castle, now a grass mound is situated to the south.

The church, founded by the hermit Meubred, was annexed to the castle of the Cardinhams at the time of the Conquest. The Cardinham family were here until the castle fell into ruins in the 14th century. Nearby are a number of antiquities, including inscribed stones, old crosses and a holy well.

Cargreen, *see* **Botus Flemming**

Carnkie, *see* **Lanner**

Carnon, *see* **Devoran**

Carpella, *see* **Nanpean**

Castallack, *see* **Lamorna**

Causeland, *see* **St Keyne**

Cawsand, *see* **Rame**

Chacewater

This once prosperous area to the west of Truro bears evidence of much former mining activity. The village has the distinction of being the place where James Watt stayed whilst installing the first pumping engines to be used in Cornish mines. *The Redruth & Chacewater Railway* opened in January 1826 and connected the mines of the Gwennap district with the port of Devoran. Anyone bemused by today's traffic hazards might pause to reflect that the place was not entirely without problems in the past. For a hundred years ago two Redruth cattle dealers were found guilty of being helplessly drunk in charge of a horse and cart in Chacewater, blocking the road, and veering this way and that. An eye witness commented drily that the horse displayed more wit and intelligence than they did.

The church of St Paul has a short and chequered history, and was once noted for its ugliness. Built in 1828, it was renovated in 1886, then damaged by lightning later that year. It was entirely rebuilt, apart from the tower in 1892, acquiring a more pleasing appearance. The east window incorporates stained glass derived from the old church of St Mary in Truro.

Charlestown

The little harbour on St Austell Bay was once crowded with tall masted brigs and schooners. Formerly known as Porthmeor, it derived its present name from Charles Rashleigh, a businessman of vision and energy, who was responsible for developing it. He engaged John Smeaton, the engineer who designed St Ives pier and the Eddystone Lighthouse, to plan the port, and the project was completed in 1801. They exported china clay, copper and tin, and imported coal, timber and other hardware. Today it remains a working port, but on a lesser scale, while most china clay is handled by Fowey and Par.

Some people felt that the design of the dock was partly to blame for the bad safety record here. In May 1862 the vessels *Margaret, Robert & Henry, Hound, Brenton* and *Katie Darling* were damaged in the harbour in the course of a south easterly gale. The schooner *John & Henry* of Ipswich left Falmouth in deteriorating conditions under the charge of a pilot, who insisted on entering harbour, despite being requested not to do so. The storm increased to a hurricane, and the vessel became a total wreck. In March 1881 the French schooner *Cecile Caroline* left here after loading with china clay, and as a fresh breeze stiffened, she was wrecked on the shore at Appletree, with the loss of her captain and crew.

Other hazards have been equally fatal. When ploughman William Pearce downed some of a local farmer's medicinal carrot seed juice, which worked wonders with the cows, he collapsed and died beside his plough. Although the inquest jury returned a verdict of 'death from natural causes', the farmer was called in and cautioned to confine his remedies to cattle in future.

Clifton, *see* **Botus Fleming**

Colan

Colan, situated on minor roads to the east of Newquay, has a small early 13th century church, set in a sheltered, leafy spot. It was once the possession of the Cardinham family, who gave it to Glasney College, near Penryn in 1276. There are 16th century brass effigies to the Bluet family and their 22 children, and to John Cosowarth, receiver general of the Duchy. Towards the end of the last century, the church was so delapidated the vicar was obliged to hold services in a loft over his stable.

On Palm Sunday, simple folk hastened to church bearing palm crosses, which were cast into the well, and gifts for the priest. If the palms floated, they took this as a sign that they would live out the year, if not, the portents were bleak.

Come-To-Good

The charmingly named village of Come-To-Good (*cum ty coit*), 'the valley by the cottage in the wood', to the south of Truro captures the imagination not only for its unusual name, but also for its pleasingly designed *Friends Meeting House*, dating from 1709, and impressive in its simplicity. It has a thatched roof, mullioned windows, plain benches and a raised gallery. George Fox, the founder of the Quakers had a rough reception when he came on a pilgrimage to Cornwall, and was thrown into Launceston gaol. Although the Quakers were greatly persecuted in earlier times, several meeting houses were established in this part of Cornwall.

Constantine

Constantine lies at the head of a creek of the Helford river estuary, well known for its oyster beds, in a particularly delightful area of hills, valleys, woods and streams. Its impressive church occupies rising ground, and commands fine views across the estuary. One vicar of Constantine met his death by falling from the roof of the church whilst supervising restoration work. The lovely old 2 storeyed schoolhouse adjoining the churchyard dates from 1733, while 1¾ miles to the north

Friends Meeting House, Come-To-Good

west is an ancient cross with a circular head and primitive style crucifix.

The area has long been famous for its quarries, and granite from Freeman's quarries was shipped from Penryn for the building of the Manchester Ship Canal, Buenos Aires harbour and Malta docks. The men working in the thirty or so quarries in the parish were on piecework, some of them dividing their time between here and America, as fluctuating opportunities allowed.

Trewardreva, originally an E-shaped manor house about a mile to the north of the village, dated from around 1600. It was remodelled in the 18th century, with additions in 1936. Opposite the entrance is Pixies Hall, an ancient long, low, underground, walled passage, known as a fogou. This may have been used for storing perishable food. It also came in handy as a cowshed and a refuge for contraband goods.

The tranquil hamlet of **Port Navas**, 1½ miles to the south east on another creek of the Helford river is also well known for its oysters.

Copperhouse, *see* **Angarrack**

Cotehele, *see* **St Dominick**

Coverack

This old world fishing village on the east coast of the Lizard, had thatched stone cottages, a little harbour and stone pier, a lifeboat station and a reputation for audacious smuggling. Today the well-tended cottages and harbour remain, and boating, bathing and tourism supplement the traditional fishing industry.

At the end of the last century, following some disastrous shipwrecks on the Manacles, it was decided that a lifeboat station should be set up to supplement the Porthoustock service on the other side of the hazardous rocks, and the lifeboat *Constance Melanie* came on station in February 1901. She and her successors performed a brave record of service in these dangerous waters, and scores of lives were saved.

Until fairly recent times, overland routes were difficult, and the Falmouth built and owned steamer *St Keverne*, specially fitted out for the passenger trade, helped farmers distribute their produce. It plied regularly between Falmouth, Helford, Durgan, Porthallow, Porthoustock and Coverack, and came into service in February 1876. The safe and dry landing arrangements also helped the tourist trade, allowing holiday makers to enjoy boating and fishing, thereby gaining a lead over its rivals.

A *Coverack Stone Company* was formed a hundred years ago to exploit stone on an extensive scale from quarries between Falmouth and the Lizard, using dynamite. It was shipped to Falmouth and Greenwich for use as hardwearing roadstone.

The local serpentine, which becomes attractive when highly polished, gave rise to a flourishing ornamental stone industry, and workshops here, as well as at Cadgwith, Mullion and Lizard have produced attractive lighthouses, ash trays, lampstands and other ornaments to grace the homes of generations of holidaymakers.

Crackington Haven, *see* **Jacobstow & St Gennys**

Crafthole, *see* **Portwrinkle**

Crantock

According to tradition, the wealthy city of Langarrow (or Languna) and its seven churches lie buried beneath the sand here. For the inhabitants, spoilt by wealth, became idle and decadent, and in time the wrath of heaven descended on them in the form of large quantities of sand. The place has certainly suffered from sand encroachment, and farmers and archaeologists have unearthed teeth and bones.

Crantock, known in earlier times as Langorroc, was important long before neighbouring Newquay, across the Gannel, even existed, for it was a thriving little coastal port in the 13th century. The village derives its name from St Carantocus, an associate of St Patrick, who landed on the shores of the Gannel, and built his oratory here by the holy well. The partly Norman church is one of the most interesting in the area. A collegiate church was founded here by Bishop Bruerne early in the 13th century with a dean and nine prebendaries, which accounts for its large chancel. In the 14th century Bishop Brantyngham drew attention to the perilous state of the tower, and left money for its restoration, but it collapsed in 1412.

The village stocks now in the churchyard, were at one time kept in the tower. A smuggler confined in them made his ingenious escape up the bell rope before making off to sea and disappearing from his Crantock home for ever. Beneath the stone floors of the *Old Albion Inn* lies a secret chamber, which played its role in local smuggling activities.

Every town and village had its fair and feast day, which offered an opportunity to escape from everyday cares. The well known Crantock Games were somewhat rumbustuously celebrated if this old rhyme is anything to go by:

'Crantock and Newlyn men all in one room,
The first gun to be shot, it proved my doom.
My name is William Coombe, just twenty in my bloom,
Just twenty when they shot me at Crantock Games.'

Creed, *see* Grampound

Crowan

The peaceful little village of Crowan, tucked away from main roads to the south of Camborne, has attractive buildings including the 19th century Church House, with massive chimney stacks and a steeply pitched roof.

The granite church of St Crewenna has numerous monuments to the St Aubyn family, who owned nearby Clowance. Its south aisle was constructed around 1710 to accommodate an influx of working miners to the area.

There was a bizarre and tragic incident at Polcrebo mine, to the south of the village, when Emanuel Jenkin, the lander, complained to the driver that his horses were not going fast enough. Whereupon he jumped up on the shafts behind the horses and urged them to greater and greater speed. As he recklessly leant out to spur them on still further, his head got caught in the mechanism, and he was killed instantly.

'Taking Day' at Clowance, offered youngsters the opportunity for romance, for after church on the Sunday preceding Praze-an-Beeble Fair (July 16th), they and others from neighbouring villages gathered for the lads to pick their partners. This was traditionally a light-hearted event, providing entertainment for onlookers as well. In 1889, thousands of folk flocked here to see the great Blondin. They were enthralled when he made his debut at the fête, wearing armour and a helmet, and performing with style and ease on a tightrope suspended 70 feet above the ground.

The old railway of 1887 linking Helston with the mainline at Gwinear Road Station skirted Crowan and made its way through mining areas which have now reverted to agriculture. There were stations at Praze and Nancegollan.

During the Great Blizzard of March 1891, the driver, his fireman, the guard and a solitary passenger were obliged to leave the train after it ran into a deep snowdrift near Polcrebo Bridge, and seek shelter at the nearby farm.

Truthall Halt, opened in 1905, was renamed Truthall Platform a year later and had a galvanised shed on a short wooden platform. Local folk relished the delights of the down gradients on the final section into Helston. This branch line was the first Cornish line to suffer from the short-sighted Beeching reorganisation, and was mourned by many when it closed in November 1962. It closed to freight traffic in October 1964.

Crows-an-Wra, *see* **St Buryan**

Crow's Nest *see* **St Cleer**

Cubert

Cubert, which derived its name from a local saint, Cubertus, is a bare, windswept village to the south of Crantock, overlooking the dunes of Penhale to the ocean beyond. Smuggling was a thriving industry here, indulged in by all layers of society. Indeed, it was placed on record that:

'Cubert's vicar
Loves good liquor.'

Cubert's little church has a broached spire on a low tower, which is unusual in Cornwall. The spire is visible for miles around. The church had to be partly rebuilt after being damaged by lightning in 1848 (see St Hilary).

The therapeutic waters of the well of St Cubertus drew hopeful folk from far and wide. It had a particular reputation for the healing of children's ailments. John Wesley visited the village several times, and was the guest of the landowning family of Hosken at Carines.

A dubious pair, Abraham Boswell, chair-mending grandson of 'Old Boswell', King of the Gipsies, and Thomas Down (alias Stanley, alias Hugal), an itinerant razor grinder, spent a moody afternoon drinking at the former Hosken's Arms, causing concern to other people. After leaving the inn, Boswell hammered Thomas to death in a nearby lane.

Streams rising near the village flow around Cubert Common to join the sea at Porth Joke. Kelsey Head beyond, is an imposing, rocky headland capped by Cliff Castle.

Cury

Cury, four miles south of Helston, and a mile inland from the sea, was the parish in which H. W. Longfellow's ancestor Richard Bonython lived before emigrating to America. The interesting church, which has a Norman south door has a 20th century window commemorating this connection.

The old man of Cury, who rescued a stranded mermaid, was granted the power to comfort fellow mortals and break evil spells. Of rather more substance is the story about a carter, who was trundling his load of furze along the lanes when he realised that it was on fire. As the flames leapt higher, he increased speed in a bid to reach a stream, increasing the air flow and making the situation worse. He managed to release the terrified horses, but the furze and the waggon became a smouldering pile of cinders.

Cury was also the home of strolling player and ballad singer Anthony James, a blind ex-soldier, who did the rounds in West Cornwall, accompanied by a boy fiddler and a dog. He made up many ballads himself as he went along the way, and some of these reflected his fascination with the supernatural. Although he wrote religious songs, his interpretation clashed with that of the Methodists, who regarded him with suspicion (see St Keverne).

Darite, *see* **Minions**

Delabole

Delabole, near Camelford, is famous for its quarry, reputedly the largest man-made hole in Britain, being 500 feet deep, with a mile and a half circumference. The distinctively beautiful slates, which polished and smooth are pleasing to the touch, have been mined here for about 600 years. Traditionally the slate was split into sizings attractively known as *Ladies, Countesses, Duchesses, Queens* and *Imperials,* and was exported all over the world, as well as being used in Cornish churches and houses for flooring and roofing. The increase of trade brought about by the arrival of the *London & South Western Railway,* caused lesser mines, dependent on horse-drawn transport and coastal vessels to close down. The influx of workers brought about the evolution of the long, straggling village, which took its name from the quarry. It encompassed the hamlets of Rockhead, Medrose and Pengelly, each of which had its own Methodist chapel.

Today the quarries are in great demand to provide the best quality British roofing slate. The material is also used for the facing of prestigious buildings, slate hanging, flooring and fireplaces. There is now a *Delabole Slate Quarry Museum,* and workers and visitors can whet their whistles at the evocatively named *Bettle & Chisel Inn.*

At nearby Lanteglos by Camelford, in a gentle landscape of hills, woods and streams, is the 14th century mother church of Camelford, beautifully situated amongst trees. In the churchyard are four old crosses, and an ancient Saxon pillar stone, discovered at the ancient fortification of Castle Goff in 1876.

The small hamlet of Trebarwith lies to the north west of Delabole. The spectacular coastline beyond, now owned by the National Trust, has been the inspiration for artists, including Creswick, who painted stormy scenes here. The strand is nearly a mile long at low tide. The road up the valley ascends between steep hillsides, clothed with flowers and bracken, and strewn with quarry debris.

De Lark, *see* **St Breward**

Devoran

Devoran, at the head of Restronguet Creek, was once a busy port, serving the mining areas of Redruth. Tin had been extracted around the River Fal from early times, and the Phoenicians may have come here in quest of it. Copper ore was brought from the Gwennap mines by packhorse and mule teams, to be exported, but the ground became waterlogged in winter and exports only gathered momentum when the *Redruth & Chacewater* Railway, which was built to a four foot gauge, came into operation around 1825. Horse traction was used until 1854, when the 0-4-0 saddle tankers Miner and Smelter came into service. Around 1905 they were joined by the locomotive Spitfire. Ships regularly plied between here and South Wales transporting ores and ingots, and returning with coal to power the mining machinery. The line closed in 1915 and was abandoned 3 years later. Parts of the track, and the remains of wharves can still be seen. The port suffered from silt, accentuated by indiscriminate dumping of waste material from the mines, and it was one of the major factors which led to its decline. However, it's an ill wind . . . The Carnon stream, which joins the tidal waters of Restronguet Creek, and which contained vast amounts of tin washed down from scores of mines in the hinter-land, presented an opportunity to be exploited. In the middle of the last century there was a large tin streaming works covering an area of the estuary a mile long, and 300 yards wide. Furthermore, the village of Carnon had extensive works for the production of arsenic from arsenical pyrites.

The way of life in these parts, when trade and communication was mostly by water, was very much geared to the working boat. In 1847, the *Redruth & Chacewater Railway Company* acquired a small, second-hand tugboat, the *Sydney,* for manoeuvring vessels around the wharves. Several of the distinctive shallow draught Truro River barges plying around these waterways were Devoran-owned. Local folk went oyster dredging during the winter months. Boatbuilding and repair yards developed around the creek – there was a particularly fine one at Point, just along the shore from Devoran. In recent times, Ralph Bird of Carnon Mine, who comes from a 'river' family, has built up a one man enterprise constructing racing gigs in the traditional style. This has not only revived a local skill, but has also given a new lease of life to a graceful and stylish sport.

Rows of handsome, substantially built terraced houses, commanding lovely views across the creek towards Carclew, were built for the workers. Carclew was the seat of William Lemon, who made a fortune from the mining industry, but unfortunately, the house, reputedly the finest in Cornwall, burnt down in 1934. In 1847 a number of young men from the Perran Foundry, having formed a cricket club and obtained permission to play in Sir Charles Lemon's park at Carclew, illicitly stretched a wire with dangling hooks across his fish pond.

Downderry

Downderry, on Whitsand Bay to the east of Looe, has many houses, bungalows and weekend retreats, many of which are suspended, boxlike, in rather unlikely situations up the steep hillside, commanding enviable coastal views.

It began as a remote little settlement of fisherfolk, who dwelt in cottages close to the shore. Evocative photographs of the last century show shawled women gathering limpets on the beach. Gradually folk from nearby towns made their way here for recreation. By 1880, people from London and further afield were attracted by the seabathing and lovely cliff walks, and there was a need for new lodging houses. Shacks mushroomed along this section of coast in the 1920s. Today it is a cheerful sort of a place, popular with holidaymakers, who enjoy its outdoor facilities.

Duloe

The village of Duloe lies on a high ridge to the north of Looe. The word 'Looe' indicates a pool, and 'Duloe' two pools. This must refer to the rivers Looe and West Looe, for the village is situated between the prongs of both. The church of St Cuby and St Leonard is interesting for its unusual plan. The well preserved, sturdy tower is attached to the south transept, and not at the west. Robert Scott, associated with the Liddell Scott Greek dictionary, was a one time rector here. Near the church is a small circle of eight stones, thirty eight feet in diameter, which may have enclosed a cairn. Cremated remains were discovered at the base of one of the stones.

St Cuby's holy well has been restored, but remains plain and simple.

Dupath, ***see*** **St Dominick**

Durgan

The unspoilt Georgian and Victorian hamlet of Durgan, now in the care of the National Trust, lies on the Helford river at the foot of wooded cliffs. The best way to see it is from the river, but it can be approached through the beautiful valley gardens of Glendurgan, or through a narrow lane (park at the top and walk down). In July 1848 the captains of foreign vessels in Falmouth harbour were brought to Glendurgan, the country seat of Alfred Fox, on the steamer *Sydney*, to enjoy cricket and other games on the lawns. A large part of Durgan and the adjoining estate of Bosveal on the Helford river was bought by Mr Pearce in the mid 1870s. Villagers put out triumphal arches, flags and decorations to greet their new landlord, as he arrived in his steam launch *Roseberry*, also gaily bedecked. He set about a programme of demolition and improvement. A capacious schoolroom was built for the children, who previously received instruction in the loft of a fish cellar. Its opening was celebrated with a tea party.

Egloshayle

Egloshayle, across the Camel from Wadebridge, was a gift of the Bishops of Exeter. Thomas Lovibond, a 15th century vicar of Egloshayle was instrumental in getting a bridge constructed over the river Camel at Wadebridge, because he considered the ferry crossing hazardous. He was supported in this venture by the money-raising activities of Courtenay, Bishop of Exeter. Thomas Lovibond was also the inspiration behind the fine tower of Egloshayle's church, pleasantly situated overlooking watermeadows.

Competition bell ringing was popular around these parts, and a song dating from 1810 commemorated the Egloshayle team thus:

'There's Craddock the Cordwainer first, that rings the treble bell,
The second is John Ellery, and none may him excell;
The third is Pollard, Carpenter, the fourth is Thomas Cleave,
Goodfellow is the tenor man, that rings them round so brave.

All five are buried in the churchyard.

Along the road to Bodmin is the pleasant village of Sladesbridge, with its slate cottages, and the whimsically named village of Washaway, which has a church built in 1882, with a pre-Norman font from Lanteglos by Camelford.

In the parish are some fine 17th century manor houses, including *Kestle*, *Croan*, built for a rich attorney, and *Pencarrow*, a fine Palladian house, dating mostly from the 18th century.

Egloskerry

Between the Kensey and Ottery rivers, to the north west of Launceston, and close to the Devon border is the village of Egloskerry, which derived its name from St Kerin, who arrived here with his three wives, concubines, 24 sons and 25 daughters, all of whom were saints. The church, occupying a central position in the village, dates from Norman times, and contains memorials to the Speccott family, who once occupied the manor house. *Penheale* is mostly 17th and 20th century, but retains a medieval window.

Feock

This exceptionally pretty village, commanding fine views down the historic Carrick Roads, recalls in its unusual name, Feoca, a contemporary of St Patrick. This is reputedly where a sermon was last preached in the Cornish language, supposedly because elderly churchgoers found difficulty understanding it in English. Of the original 13th century church, only the single-storeyed west tower remains, and today it stands detached from the present, mostly 19th century church. There is an attractive early 19th century lych gate, with a slate hung upper storey, probably used as a vestry or schoolroom.

A steam ferry at King Harry Passage, which replaced the old horse-drawn boat in 1889, had the advantage of being able to make crossings at any state of the tide, whatever the weather. It ran every quarter of an hour, taking 3¾ minutes. Today a modern car ferry links the Roseland peninsula with the western shores.

Trelissick House, (National Trust) is reckoned to be the finest Palladian mansion in the county and has enchanting gardens sweeping down to the riverbanks, delightful at all seasons. An advertisement of 1890 sought a cycling messenger from Truro to deliver the Trelissick mailbag every morning for the payment of eight shillings a week.

Flushing

Across the water from Falmouth's Greenbank, and accessible by passenger ferry from the *Prince of Wales Pier*, is this delightful, picturesque village. Founded by the Dutch in the 17th century, and constructed on faggots because of swampy subsoil, it became a place of style and refinement, where the captains of the packets and their families lived. Today the village still retains that touch of class, with its tastefully renovated 17th and 18th century houses. In contrast the church of St Peter is relatively new, dating only from 1842. In conditions of exceptionally high tide, some of the village has been subject to flooding, allowing boats to take to the streets.

West of Flushing is Little Falmouth, where several of the packets were built. In April 1874, the large barque *Charlotte Padbury* was launched from H. S. Trethowan's yard here. She had a 50 feet poop, spacious decks, eight state rooms for passengers and two private cabins, and was built for the Australian run. Today Flushing is a centre for fishing and sailing, and stages colourful regattas, where the graceful old working boats add a touch of authenticity to the changing nautical scene.

An appalling tragedy occurred at nearby Trefusis Point in January 1814, when the transport *Queen*, returning home with invalided soldiers, women and children, was driven onto the rocks in a terrific storm, with the loss of 195 lives.

Forrabury, *see* **Boscastle**

Four Lanes, *see* **Wendron**

Fraddon, *see* **Retew**

Gear, *see* **Gweek**

Germoe

Germoe, between Helston and Marazion has a quaint and attractive little church of Norman origin, enlarged and rebuilt in the 15th century, with a pinnacled and battlemented tower. The well, mentioned by early historians, has vanished, unlike the strange two pillared structure in the churchyard, known as St Germoe's Chair which may have been an altar tomb.

After the unsaintly behaviour of St Keverne and St Just (see St Keverne), the rocks hurled after the latter are said to have landed in a field here, thereafter known as Tremen Keverne, 'The Three Stones of Keverne.'

Bizarre legends surround *Pengersick Castle* at Para Sands, to the south. Late medieval, embattled, with a tower and once the seat of the Milliton family, it is said to have been built for a wealthy merchant, and was later taken over by a fugitive, who took refuge here after committing murder in London. Here also dwelt another wicked man, who went abroad to fight, forgot his marriage vows and seduced the daughter of a king. Having been deserted by him, she followed him to Cornwall with her small son, but was cruelly cast into the sea by this false lover. The boy was rescued and returned many years later to claim his inheritance. The princess died, and her spirit entered the body of a white hare, which frightened her former lover's horse when he was out hunting, causing it to bolt into the sea, drowning itself and its rider.

Gerrans

The pleasing village of Gerrans is situated on the eastern side of the Roseland Peninsula, just inland from Portscatho. 'Roseland', although encompassing one of Cornwall's mildest and most enchantingly flowery regions, derives its name not from roses but 'Rosinis', or 'moorland isle'. Although the church of St Gerent has an appearance of antiquity, it was entirely rebuilt in 1849, apart from the tower, using the original stones and windows. It has a Norman font, a Celtic cross in the churchyard, and a spire that has been a landmark to generations of seafarers.

The area is where Gerannius, mythical King of Cornwall had his palace of Dingerein, said to have been connected to the shore by an underground passage known as the Mermaid's Hole. According to legend, his body was rowed across the heavenly Gerrans Bay in a golden boat with silver oars, and he was buried with his crown, sword and full regalia in the boat, beneath Carne Beacon, near Veryan.

The village commands breathtaking views across the bay, towards Gull Rock and Nare Head, which has been the scene of many a shipwreck. (see Portscatho). On the eastern side of the bay is a fine example of a raised beach, built by the waves when the sea stood at a higher level, relative to the land.

Gillan, *see* Manaccan

Godolphin Cross, *see* Breage

Golant

Trees, flowers and pleasing cottages characterise the little village on the western banks of the Fowey river, which has associations with Charles I and Arthurian legend.

The small church of St Sampson, who was a 6th century saint from Glamorgan, was consecrated in 1509 and has a holy well beside the south porch.

Unfortunately, the passenger railway which used to carry little steam trains so picturesquely along the edge of the water was closed in the 1960s but English China Clay International waggon trains now ply this route and the sheltered pool once filled with beautiful work-a-day vessels now provides a haven for pleasure craft. The contractors encountered many difficulties building the Lostwithiel to Carne Point section of railway, started in 1863, particularly at Golant Downs. For it had long been traditional for the impoverished villagers to enjoy grazing rights, and on an appointed day once a year they were allowed to take as much fern for fuel as they could carry on their backs. This meant that the company was obliged to serve notices on every claimant to end his rights.

The area was traditionally associated with the romance of Tristram and Iseult, and the grassy mound known as Castle Dore was reputedly the palace of King Mark, legendary King of Cornwall. It was also regarded as a possible venue of the Knights of the Round Table. Charles I slept overnight in his carriage here in 1644, before the surrender of Lord Essex.

Goldsithney

Goldsithney, a village on the Camborne to Marazion road, has long been noted for its annual fair on August 5th, and for its fine views across Mount's Bay from the Goldsithney hills. The large cattle fair held here came about as the result of Goldsithney folk casting envious eyes on Sithney's fair, and making off with its traditional, symbolic glove, of the type used at Chester. At one time it was customary to pay an annual conscience fee of one shilling to Sithney, in lieu of past (un)fair dealings.

In September, 1855 to celebrate the fall of Sebastapol, the young men of Relubbus in St Hilary marched through Goldsithney to Marazion, bearing an effigy of the Emperor of Russia, lit up with candles and mounted on a long pole. They were accompanied by a band of musicians, and twenty guns were fired at intervals along the route (see Mevagissey).

Gorran

The little village of Gorran, a mile inland from Gorran Haven, and 300 feet above sea level, clusters around its imposing 15th century church, itself well known to generations of mariners. Opposite its entrance is the handsome, granite Georgian Barley Sheaf inn, and not far away is the windswept school immortalised in Anne Treneer's autobiographical story *Schoolhouse In the Wind,* published in 1944, which captured the essence of everyday village life (a sequel *Cornish Years,* was published in 1949). St Gorran Penny Clothing Society, founded in 1839, offered an opportunity for the poor to acquire subsidised secondhand clothing and bedding for subscriptions of a penny a week. Some of the villagers fished as a livelihood, but most worked on the farms. The annual Turnip Hoeing Championship drew sixty to seventy local entries as well as a large number of appreciative spectators, and competition was keen between Gorran men and their neighbours from St Ewe. Ten yoked oxen were still in use at nearby Bodrugan Farm at the end of the last century, and bees thrived on the flowers and white clover which grew in the fields and hedgerows.

An old Gorran rhyme relates:

'I met a fellow, clothed in yellow,
Upon a cloudy day;
I picked him up, and sucked his blood,
Then threw his skin away . . .'

But fortunately it was about nothing more sinister than an orange.

It is said that the Wise Men of Gorran, (or Towednack or Zennor or St Agnes) built a hedge around a cuckoo in an attempt to preserve eternal spring. They once attempted to catch the moon's reflection in a bucket of water, which they then threw over a cliff in the hope that it would improve the weather which had been ruining the harvest.

Gorran Haven

This small fishing settlement between Chapel Point and the Dodman was formerly known as Porthjust. St Goren or Goronus is said to have been a hermit from Bodmin.

There was once bitter rivalry between the Gorran fishermen and the Mevagissey fishermen. In 1873 the Gorran men complained that their Mevagissey counterparts had sunk their pots and towed them far out to sea, while they were accused of cutting the Mevagissey men's drift nets, and sinking them with stone weights. (On one occasion they cut their own nets by mistake!) Gorran fishermen were wholly dependent on crabbing to support their wives and families.

An old Cornish proverb would have us believe that we can achieve the impossible only when Rame Head and the Dodman meet. Some say that this happened when both lands came into the possession of the Edgcumbe family. The name 'Dodman' for this prominent point may have been derived from Dodmaen, meaning a stony prominence. Romantics opt for the 'Dead man' derivation, citing the legendary giant who met a sad end here, and the many hapless victims of shipwrecks. The Dodman rises steeply from the sea over 370 feet and is traversed by a long, defensive earthwork. A massive cross on the top was erected by the rector of St Michael Caerhayes as a daymark for shipping. This was the setting for Sir Arthur Quiller Couch's novel *Dead Man's Rock*. Chapel Point is similarly capped by an ancient fort. Both headlands are in the care of the National Trust, and command some of the loveliest coastal views in Cornwall.

Grampound

Grampound is situated on the upper reaches of the River Fal, and was on the main medieval highway westwards. Its name is derived from 'grand pont' or 'great bridge', for it represented a symbol of status. A street grew up along the approaches to the bridge, and it received its first charter in 1332. It was an age when many such boroughs were being founded as a means of deriving revenue through market tolls, fair tolls and urban rents. The burgesses were prepared to pay highly for these privileges, and the crown was happy to accept their money. This was one of seven villages in the Duchy of Cornwall to be made a borough, and enfranchised during the reign of Edward VI, to ensure that the men returned to Parliament were supportive of the monarchy. Grampound sent members to Parliament for nearly three hundred years.

Cornwall was notorious for its rotten and pocket boroughs, the most flagrant of which were disenfranchised in the 1832 Reform Bill. However, Grampound had the dubious distinction of being so corrupt that it had to be disenfranchised before the rest, by the Special Act of 1821

The cottages alongside the single street of the main road today provide a pleasing reminder of the nature of a traditional small town. The chapel of ease, built in 1869, occupies the site of an ancient church, dedicated to St Non. There is a market place with a medieval cross, a Guildhall and clock-tower, and opposite is Croggon's Manor Tannery, which still uses oak bark for tanning.

This area of ancient settlements was a parish before the church was built. The whimsical story goes that a giant, unaware of his own strength, hurled a stone to determine the site for the church. He threw with such gusto, that the stone almost went beyond the parish limits; which accounts for Grampound's parish church being at Creed, a mile to the south, and little more than a hamlet. At nearby Golden Farm, the priest, Cuthbert Mayne was seized for ministering Catholicism to leading families at a time of religious suppression. He was executed at Launceston, in 1577 and was later beatified by Leo XII.

The settlement at Grampound Road grew up around the railway station.

Gulval

Gulval, overlooking Mount's Bay, is a pleasing village of well-tended Victorian cottages and houses. The church contains many memorials to the influential and bountiful Bolitho family, and in the churchyard is the intriguing Pirate's Grave, surrounded by legend and mystery. Gulval's holy well, which was one of the best known in Cornwall, had a reputation as a divining well, and anxious girls could seek news of absent lovers by gazing into its waters and chanting:

'Water, water, tell me truly,
Is the man that I love duly
On the earth, or under the sod,
Sick or well, in the name of God?'

and hope that the water would be clear, rather than troubled and cloudy.

Oreweed, or seaweed, was gathered as a fertilizer from nearby Mount's Bay by farmers in boats, using scythes fixed to long poles. Early spring flowers and vegetables have long been grown on the fertile, south facing slopes, whole families tilling the small fields together.

One observer wrote that, 'The use of the long handled spade necessitates attitudes of classic grace,' a pose more appreciated by the spectator than the wielder, no doubt. Springtime saw the colourful results of their labours, when, it was said, the air was heavy with the scent of flowers, which were carefully packed, and sent by rail from Penzance to London.

Mead, that agreeable age old tipple mentioned in historical literature, was revived by the monks here, and the *Blessing of the Mead* was carried out on 24th August, the day of St Bartholomew, patron saint of beekeepers and honeymakers. Another rather unlikely product of these parts during the last century was artificially produced ice for Newlyn's fishing industry.

In 1814, the last public bull-baiting was carried out in the parish, in a field near Ponsandane bridge, when a large and enthusiastic crowd watched the unfortunate bull led in by four men. But when a violent thunderstorm broke out the crowd dispersed rapidly – some thinking the storm to be judgement from On High.

Two miles north of Gulval is the Iron Age fort of Castle an Dinas, incorporating a folly known as Roger's Tower which was erected by a local landowner in 1798. This is an area exceptionally rich in archaeological interest, with inscribed stones, Bodrifty Iron Age settlement, standing stones and the ancient village of Chysauster, incorporating the best preserved group of courtyard houses in Cornwall.

Gunnislake

The Tamar river, which divides Cornwall from Devon, meanders its way southwards in huge loops, and flows past Gunnislake before joining other rivers to reach the sea through Plymouth Sound. The New Bridge, a beautiful granite structure 182 feet long, with seven arches, constructed around 1520 by Sir Piers Edgcumbe of Cotehele, is considered to be one of Cornwall's finest. For centuries it was the principal entry into Cornwall, and as such was hotly contested at the time of the Civil War.

Gunnislake, straggling up the steep hillside from the bridge, was a boom village in the hey-day of mining, for this was one of the richest areas, producing tin, copper, wolfram and arsenic. The *East Cornwall Mineral Railway*, which opened in 1872, linked the mines and quarries with Calstock Quay. It was taken over by the *Plymouth, Devonport & South Western Junction Railway*, who constructed the viaduct in 1907.

Grey and white cottages hug the hillsides at Calstock above the tidal river flanked by reedbeds. There was a limekiln here and a brickworks just across the Devon border. Calstock Quay was formerly busy handling material from the mines and local farms. The place has retained an individual charm, and also its rail links with Plymouth and Gunnislake. Between Gunnislake and Calstock the river winds between steeply wooded banks, past the restored Morwellham Quay, on the Devon side, now a popular tourist attraction.

A long standing feud between miners Richard Piper and John Bodiner reached a tragic conclusion in nearby Latchley in November 1860, when they adjourned from the *Rising Sun* to a neighbouring field to sort out their differences with a two hour bout of fisticuffs, which ended with John Bodiner being killed by a blow from Richard Piper, who emerged mangled and almost blinded.

Hingston Down, to the west, was the centre of a mining area, and in olden times Cornish and Devon miners met here every seven or eight years. On this exposed site a windmill, which once powered the mines, was destroyed by the very power it harnessed. This was also the site of a battle between combined Cornish and Danish forces, who lost to the Saxon Egbert in A.D. 835. Kit Hill, 1091 feet high, topped by the tall stack of a derelict mine offers one of the most outstanding vantage points of the South West.

Gunwalloe

If Gunwalloe, on the west coast of the Lizard has a name with a rollicking ring, colourful events have matched that expectation, for it is associated with storms, shipwrecks, smuggling and buried treasure. Its romantically situated church, in the lee of the sand dunes, and subject to salty spray from the sea, is said to have been built as a thanks offering for survival from shipwreck. Ironically the bodies of shipwrecked soldiers and sailors washed up on the nearby Halzephron shores early in the last century were refused burial in consecrated ground, and were thrown *en masse* into a pit in a field. This created such an outcry that an Act of Parliament sanctioned the burial of shipwrecked victims in the nearest churchyard. It became customary to hold services here on All Saints Day for those lost at sea and this churchyard was the last resting place for a number of them.

The first church, built in 570, was dedicated to the Breton saint, Winwaloe. The present church was rebuilt in the 14th and 15th centuries, and a detached belfry of an older church, built into the solid rock, has two storeys and a pyramidal roof.

The buccaneer John Emery was believed to have buried his ill-gotten treasure in the local sand dunes, before setting sail on what proved to be his last voyage. In 1526, a Portuguese ship carrying copper, silver, plate, precious stones, jewels and chests full of money, was wrecked here. Three local magistrates, who hurried to the scene with their retainers in tow, claimed to have gone there to help the victims. When asked what had become of the £10,000 worth of bounty known to have been recovered, they insisted that they had only made £20 out of it, and that had been given by the captain in return for their help. The King of Portugal's appeals were in vain. Stories of unclaimed treasure led John Knill, Collector of Customs of St Ives to organise a search in 1770, but it was fruitless. After another wreck in 1785, coins were washed up. In 1845 a dam was constructed, and water drained out, in an attempt to make the sands yield up the coins, but the whole thing was broken up by storms before much was recovered.

Gweek

This old port, at the head of the Helford river, was on the trading routes from early times. The Phoenicians may have come here in quest of tin, and the Romans had an encampment at nearby Gear. After Helston suffered a set-back in trading because of the build-up of Loe Bar, Gweek flourished and became the leading port in the area. Mining material from Wendron was brought here to be exported, coal and timber for the mines was imported. The Truro river barges called here regularly, until just after the last war. In common with the Fal, the decline of waterborne trade was hastened by the silting up of the river as the result of waste material from the mines being deposited upstream.

Old photographs of tall masted ships in this hauntingly beautiful creek give some insight into its former importance and work-a-day charm. It was the setting for Hereward's Cornish adventures, as related by Charles Kingsley. But there were those who set their sights on a better way of life overseas. An advertisement of 1837 ran thus: 'The Fast sailing ship *Caroline* of Gweeke, John Broad, Commander, A.1, copper fastened, burthen 400 tons, will positively sail, wind and weather permitting, from Gweeke for Philadelphia, on Monday, the 27th day of March instant, with Passengers only. For particulars apply at the Office of Messrs. Cornish and Borlase, at Gweeke; or to Mr J. H. Edwards, General Commissioned Agent, Camborne.'

In the middle of the last century, William Johns of Gweek, horse trainer, rough rider and riding instructor, proudly proclaimed that he was 'open in the saddle against any man in the kingdom at 112 lbs weight.'

Today there is a seal sanctuary at Gweek, where seals, birds, porpoises, dolphins and turtles washed up on the Cornish coast are cared for.

Gwennap

Gwennap, to the south east of Redruth is generally associated with

John Wesley and Methodism, and it originated as a mining settlement in one of the richest mining areas in the country. There were miles of underground tunnels, and some of the mines reached a depth of over 1,700 feet, only ladders giving access to the shafts. It is small wonder that fatalities were high, life expectancy short.

John Wesley came to the village to preach in 1743, but first preached in Gwennap Pit in 1762. He relished its acoustics and the crowds, and returned several times last preaching here in his 85th year. The Pit, some distance from the village, is a stepped amphitheatre, 300 yards in circumference, and probably created by mining subsidence.

On Whit Monday in 1859 huge crowds gathered at the Pit from all over the county. Enterprising youngsters offered to keep an eye on waiting horses – if the price was right, while the carriage passengers savoured the spiritual experience, not to mention the gingerbread cakes and other temptations displayed on the many stalls which had somehow mushroomed overnight. Gwennap Pit was also used for wrestling, cock fighting and the production of miracle plays, often with music and dancing.

Although this was the hub of Cornwall's richest mining area, here, as in the Perran, St Agnes, Lelant, St Ives, Helston, Breage and other mining districts, it was a case of 'knack'd bals' (defunct mines) by the mid 1890s. (see St Agnes, St Day, Lanner, St Michael Caerhayes, Scorrier).

Twelveheads, in the parish of Gwennap, was the birthplace of Billy Bray, (1794-1868) an illiterate miner, and disciple of John Wesley, who went around the county preaching in a similarly compelling style. It was also the home of Martin Oates, who was blinded in an accident in a copper mine,and became a familiar figure in local towns, trying to eke out a living playing a violin and singing hymns.

Gwinear

Gwinear's station was about a mile away. It was known as Gwinear Road Station and established in 1843 when the *Hayle Railway* introduced its passenger service. This was taken over by the *West Cornwall Railway Company* in 1846, and by the *Great Western Railway Company* in 1878. It was chosen as the mainline junction with the *Helston Railway*, and had up and down platforms on the main line as well as a platform for the branch line, and a siding where vegetables were loaded for the up-country markets. The Helston branch line closed to passengers in 1962, much to the regret of many who came to witness its sad ending. There were two signal boxes known as Gwinear Road

East and Gwinear Road West, and it had the distinction of possessing the longest level crossing gates in Cornwall, replaced by automatic barrier gates in 1965. Back in 1852 some enterprising, not to say drunk villagers, found themselves in trouble for placing a truck on the newly constructed railway line, and borrowing a donkey from a nearby farm to draw them home, after the last train had left.

The grey village, with its ancient church is situated in windswept farming country with few trees in an area of scattered hamlets. Nearby Lanyon dates from 1668. In olden times this was the seat of the family of that name, one of whom, Captain Lanyon, accompanied Captain Cook on his voyages around the world. Polkinghorne Farm, a quarter

Men-an-Tol, Lanyon

of a mile west is 17th century, with later additions. Rosewarne was once in the possession of the Arundells of Lanherne, and an aisle in the church is named after them.

Roseworthy, just to the north of the village, has one of the county's earliest chapels, now extended. It is of pleasing design, single storeyed, and thatched, with Georgian windows.

Gwithian

The mighty Atlantic rollers pound these eastern shores of St Ives Bay, and explode into surf and spray. Here the wind blew sands and created towans over the ancient oratory near the Red River, and threatened the village. Gwithian Towans cover the site of an extensive Bronze Age farm, where excavations revealed huts and fields of the 5th and 6th centuries. We now know that the inhabitants kept cows, pigs, sheep, horses and dogs, worked a cross system of ploughing, used iron and made pottery. At Connor Downs, a pattern of bigger, more recent square and rectangular enclosures has been identified, while at Crane Godrevy, a mile to the north, is the remains of a small and ancient manor, incorporated into a small, fortified, Late Iron Age enclosure. It is said that the earthworks, known as Trevarnon Round, was last used in the Civil War.

The Irish Saint Gwithian landed here around 490, and built a church. The Irish influence in this area is explained by its proximity to Hayle, which was the port of disembarkation for the Irish in those early days. The charming village to which he left his name, with its 15th century church, chapel, Victorian inn, attractive cottages and bent over trees, lies in a windswept situation behind the dunes.

Godrevy Island, with its distinctive white lighthouse, inspired Virginia Woolf's novel *To The Lighthouse*. She wrote of her childhood experiences in this much loved area, when she stayed at Talland House in St Ives. It is said she was a demon bowler in family cricket matches. The area has great atmosphere.

On the day Charles I was beheaded in January 1649 a storm caused a section of Land's End to topple and dragged the vessel *Garland*, carrying the King's belongings from her moorings at St Ives onto the rocks of Godrevy. There have been numerous other shipwrecks, with great loss of life, but it was the wrecking of the *Nile* in November 1854, that caused a public outcry about the need for a lighthouse and which led to its construction. In 1858 the men who were building it were cut off from the mainland by storms, and although they had adequate shelter and a good supply of coal they suffered from hunger and thirst. At the beginning of 1890, the storms were such that the relief became more than seven weeks overdue. Today the lighthouse is automated. The rugged coastline between Navax Point and Portreath has a mixture of romantic and grim names, such as Fishing Cove, Hell's Mouth, Deadman's Cove, Crane Islands, Samphire Head and Ralph's Cupboard, reflecting its colourful ecology, shipwrecks, smuggling and other maritime happenings.

Hampt, *see* **Stoke Climsland**

Helebridge, *see* **Marhamchurch)**

Helford

The best way to savour this area is from the water, and trips from Falmouth run up the Helford river for much of the year. Approaching up-river one sees the delightfully situated Mawnan church on the starboard side with Parson's Beach below, and the village and gardens of Durgan, before reaching Helford Passage, which is linked by ferry to Helford village on the southern shores. Half a mile westwards is the hauntingly beautiful Frenchman's Creek, a long winding inlet, immortalised in Daphne du Maurier's romantic novel. The quiet, secluded tree-fringed Helford River was once nicknamed 'Stealford' river on account of being much frequented by pirates.

Helford was formerly a busy work-a-day place, described by Daniel Defoe in the 1730s as 'a small but good harbour, where many times the tin ships go in to load for London.'

In the last century there were side paths for horse traffic, and it was commonplace to see drovers swimming their stock across the river in the traditional manner. The passenger ferry was summoned by hailing or running a flag up the flagpole, but such were the complaints about the state of the ferries that 'few persons care to brave the danger of transit, choosing rather to walk round Gweek (a distance of ten miles), than expose themselves to the double risk of being detained in wet and cold, and crossing in such dangerous boats.'

Helford has not changed much since it was described a hundred years ago as 'a picture of peace and flowers,' where roses bloomed over cottage windows, fuchsias overtopped the houses, colourful flowers grew on cottage walls and the plum trees promised a good harvest.

Hendra, ***see*** **St Dennis & Nanpean**

Henwood

Henwood lies at the edge of Bodmin moor, to the west of the Lynher river, in an area rich in pre-history. To the north west lies Kilmar Tor, above the romantically named Twelve Men's Moor. In 1856 the Cheesewring Granite Company took a lease on the Kilmar Granite Sett from the Duchy, and the Kilmar Railway was opened in August 1858. It joined the Cheesewring branch at Minions. However, the Kilmar Railway only had a short working life.

The loose rock was loaded directly onto the railway waggons by ramps or from platforms alongside the track. These have now disappeared. The terminus of the railway near Kilmar Tor extended as quarrymen moved to new surface deposits.

Herodsfoot

This charming little village to the south west of Liskeard, in a steep upper combe, where two tributaries of the West Looe River meet, was the tranquil setting for the establishment of the East Cornwall Gunpowder Company in 1846. In August 1854 there was a loud early morning explosion as the drying and packing houses blew up, and roofs and windows of nearby buildings disintegrated. The cause was thought to have been a workman going into the drying house to check the temperature, carrying a spark from the fireplace on his trousers. He ran and took cover in a ditch, and escaped with just a few bruises. (see Perranwell).

Hessenford

There is a lovely drive or walk from the mouth of the Seaton River, up through the wooded valley to the unspoilt village of Hessenford, attractively situated at the intersection of two tributaries, amid woods and grassy slopes. The village has dark slate cottages, an inn and a church built in the middle of the last century, dedicated to St Anne. As this had no bells, a nocturnal salute to nuptial joy in 1850 was celebrated by the discharging of firearms, much to the annoyance of the minister, who found it difficult to identify the offenders. Being of a somewhat philosophical turn of mind, he hit on the down-to-earth notion of getting a policeman to act as a spy in the village beerhouse, and in this way one Robert Chiswell found himself in the dock answering charges at Torpoint Petty Sessions.

One Hessenford cow who broke her leg was spared the trip to the knacker's yard. Instead her leg was amputated below the knee joint, and she was fitted with a wooden one.

Holmbush, *see* **Charlestown**
Holywell, *see* **Perranporth**

Indian Queens

Cornwall was well to the fore in the construction of turnpike roads, having had the route established in connection with the Falmouth Post Office Packet Service from Falmouth to Grampound via Truro as early as 1754. With sections further eastward completed, a road was authorised from a point to the south of Launceston to the inn called the Indian Queens in 1769 giving a direct route over the moors. It was an important thoroughfare carrying the bulk of the mail and passengers to West Cornwall, and it remains as today's busy A30.

The place took its name from that old posting inn, but how the inn derived its name is less clear. Some say that a travelling Indian queen stayed here, and others subscribe to the theory that it was slept in by Pocohontas, the Red Indian Chief's daughter, who saved the life of John Smith in Virginia, and who came to London in 1616 as the Christian wife of Thomas Rolfe. However, there is no evidence that she ever set foot in Cornwall, and the name may reflect the 18th century penchant for importing foreigners as servants or curiosities, as a stylish status symbol, which led to incorporating their names in locations. Colloquially the place is known as 'Queens'.

In April 1854 Indian Queens got a foretaste of the future, in the form of a mammoth traffic jam clogging the approach roads to Bodmin. The great attraction responsible was the public hanging of a murderer at Bodmin.

The River Fal rises on nearby Goss Moor, flows through the china clay landscape, and eventually makes its majestic way down Carrick Roads to the sea.

Jacobstow

Jacobstow, on secondary routes just east of the Bude to Boscastle road, lies in one of Cornwall's lesser known inland agricultural areas, characterised by fields, trees, scattered farms, tracks, lanes and a number of streams. Some flow through steep combes into Bude Bay, while the young River Ottery makes its way south eastwards towards Launceston, to eventually become a part of the impressive Tamar, that symbol of Cornish independence.

For those who care for unfrequented places and quiet walks, there is a variety of inland footpaths, while other paths embrace the dramatic coastline and combes of Millook and Crackington Haven.

This pretty, unspoilt place, thought to have its roots in Saxon times, has a church, pleasantly situated, and dedicated to St James, with a massive Norman font of Tintagel greenstone, and a pulpit fashioned from ancient benchends. The registers date back to 1653. Jacobstow was the birthplace of Digory Weare, in 1573, who was author of several works, including *A Life of Camden*.

Kea (Old Kea & Porth Kea)

The Irish Saint Kea or Kenan, converted by St Patrick, came floating to Cornwall on a granite boulder, so it was said, and his point of happy landing was once known as Landegea, meaning 'Church of the Blessed Ke.' All that remains of Old Kea church is the tower, now an atmospheric, romantic ruin, open to the skies, and much favoured by birds and other wildlife. This church was replaced by another in 1802, designed by James Wyatt, and described in Murray's Hand-Book of 1865 as being 'more like a riding school than a church in appearance'. This was replaced yet again at the end of the century by the present church designed by G. H. Fellowes Prynne. It has a lead spire and steep, tiled roof, and has been described by Pevsner as 'very un-Cornish, but attractive.'

The parish of Kea, which is dissected by the main road from Truro to Falmouth, verged on the mining areas, but was agricultural, dependent on its trade by water. Kea has long been famous for its plums, which grow so well on the sunny slopes of Coombe and Cowlands Creek. The spring blossom is glorious, whilst in August visitors used to come by steamer to watch the locals at work picking and sorting. The fruit was placed in fern lined baskets, and was taken by boat to

Truro and Falmouth, to be sold in the markets. The menfolk apportioned their year between plum growing, oyster dredging, and 'barking' the oak trees on Lord Falmouth's estates, to obtain resin for use in the leather industry. Mineral ore, used in the preparation of paint, and in the process of staining paper, was produced here.

An old legend told of a crock of gold found beneath the old stone cross, which was removed from the finder's possession by the landowner, who thereafter was unable to keep stock on his land, unless the animals were branded with the protective sign of the cross keys.

The name 'Killiow', to the west of the main road near the 'new'church, denoted a secluded place of refuge. It became the seat of the Daubuz family. The square, granite residence was restored in the 18th and 19th centuries, and has a coach house.

Kilkhampton

This attractive, windswept village 600 feet above sea level, in a sparsely populated area to the north of Stratton, is notable for its imposing church tower and its associations with the Grenville family. The church's beautiful Norman door, considered by some to be the best in Cornwall, probably dates from about 1150, whilst its much-prized baroque organ is rumoured to be that on which the great composer Henry Purcell played in Westminster Abbey. The church also contains exceptional wood carvings, and monuments to the Grenvilles. On the porch are the arms of John Grenville, Rector, with the date 1567, and the words *Porta Celi*. This church, with its churchyard was the inspiration for Harvey's *Meditations Among The Tombs*.

Originally this was a Celtic settlement, and traces still remain of the cultivation strips which surrounded it. Interestingly, the Celtic name 'Kilk' had the English 'hampton' added to it, which is rather unusual. A prehistoric trackway from Mount's Bay crossed the Carnmenellis area, Hensbarrow Down and Bodmin Moor, to connect with up-country routes near Kilkhampton. This avoided the need to cross the Tamar.

The two storey *Aldercombe*, mostly 17th century, but dating from earlier times has mullioned windows and a fine Tudor arched gateway. Three miles to the west of the village was *Stowe*, built by John Grenville, Earl of Bath, in 1680, and described by Borlase as the noblest house in the west of England. However, this masterpiece was pulled down in 1739, and only the former stables remain. The entire contents and fabric were sold, and it was said that there was not a West Country house which did not have something from *Stowe*. The place was mentioned in Charles Kingsley's *Westward Ho!* The first Grenville in our history was cousin to William the Conqueror. Other famous members of the family include the Elizabethan Sir Richard, hero of the *Revenge*, and Sir Bevil, heroic loyalist of the Civil War.

A moorland stream makes its delightful way through the steeply wooded gorge of Coombe Valley to the spectacular coast. A cottage here provided another inspirational place, where R. S. Hawker wrote his famous *Trelawny* ballad, which he originally claimed to have discovered, and wished to be regarded as authentic. It commemorated the imprisonment and trial of the Seven Bishops, in 1688, among them Sir Jonathan Trelawny of *Trelawne*.

Ladock

One of the early routes into West Cornwall passed through the beautiful wooded Ladock valley, and the road was surfaced with Cornish greenstone in the last century. Ladock's *Falmouth Arms* was one of a series of coaching inns along the way, where horses could be changed. Local folk who could afford a shilling, could take the 'Inkerman' van to Truro on market day. The rather uncomfortable seven mile journey took two hours each way.

At one time it was thought to be a right that anyone who built a house in one night could claim its freehold, and several people in Ladock achieved this seemingly impossible feat. It was also customary here to enjoy a good meal set out on long tables on tithe paying day, but this custom had died out by 1890. Quantities of tin were produced here, and this was where the largest lumps of gold were discovered in Cornwall.

The church of St Ladoca was rededicated in 1268 by Bishop Bronescombe, and restored in 1864. Parson Woods of Ladock, one of Cornwall's best layer of ghosts, was a familiar figure around these parts during the 18th century, stalking around with his ebony and silver walking stick, decorated with mystical signs and meaningful figures. But this was no ordinary walking stick, for the reverend gentleman had hit on the novel idea of changing evil spirits into animals, then whipping the living daylights out of them. Bemused and frightened parishioners who stumbled across him as he thrashed his way around the churchyard after dark, were liable to come in for a bit of stick as well. In 1837 Miss Miners of Ladock, who was bitten by an adder, was charmed by Mrs Davies of St Stephen in Branwell, and cured immediately.

Lamorran, *see* **Ruan Lanihorne**

Lamorna

The haunting beauty of Lamorna Cove attracted artists long before they colonised St Ives, and it is now most closely associated with S. J. Lamorna Birch, one of the Newlyn School of painters, who had a cottage here.

The little harbour was built for the export of granite from the nearby quarries, but fell into disuse because of difficulties in getting vessels in and out along this notoriously dangerous stretch of coast. The granite extracted here was of high quality, and a single block of it, twenty two feet high was sent to the Great Exhibition of 1851 in London. Lamorna granite was used for buildings throughout southern England, particularly in London, and for the construction of the Thames Embankment and Dover's Admiralty Pier.

On one occasion some casks of gunpowder being transported from the Penzance rail terminus to the quarries on a stone waggon exploded, throwing the driver forward with his clothes ablaze, and tearing the waggon to pieces.

Local fishermen believed in mermaids or 'merrymaids', and some thought that seals were really mermaids. At Mermaid's Rock, a lady with the tail of a fish, supposedly sat with a comb and a glass in her hand, as detailed in that rousing and romantic shanty *The Mermaid*.

On the cliffs at nearby Castallack are traces of Iron Age cattle pounds with medieval modifications. In contrast is Tater du, Britain's first remote control lighthouse, erected in 1968, close the the point of the Penlee lifeboat disaster in December 1981, when the entire crew was lost whilst going to the aid of the *Union Star*.

Landewednack (Church Cove)

There are no signposts to lead you to the tiny village of Landewednack, on the eastern tip of the Lizard above Church Cove. Its church of St Winwalloe, protectively situated amid trees, has the distinction of being the most southerly in the country. It is constructed of the local blue-green, velvety black Lizard serpentine stone. Some say that the last sermon in the Cornish language was preached here in 1678. (See Feock) Shipwreck victims, and those who died of the plague in 1645 are buried in the churchyard.

It was an old Shrove Tuesday custom for children to make their cheery way around the parish crying:

'Hen cock, han cock,
Give me a tabban, (morsel)
Or Col-perra shall
Come to your door.'

And they were given food or coins.

Landrake

This village on the Lynher, to the north west of Saltash, has a church dating from Norman times, when local freestone was much easier to fashion using basic pick and axe, than granite. Its 100 feet tower creates a landmark for miles around.

On May Day morning, it was a custom to thrash with stinging nettles anyone found languishing in bed after 6.00 a.m. Girls around the local villages would be up and gathering ferns, for if their fronds were large enough to cover the cream bowl, they would chant:

'Here's a fern to measure your shern,
Please give me some milk and cream!'

And they would be rewarded with slices of bread and cream.

Landulph, *see* **Botus Fleming**

Laneast, *see* **Alternun**

Lanivet

Lanivet, to the south west of Bodmin, on the coaching route, claims to be the central point of Cornwall and is particularly interesting for its ancient relics. Lanivet Quoit consists of three stones, one of which was an enormous capstone. Possibly dating from the 5th century are a Latin inscribed pillar stone by the south porch of the church, a cross slab in the churchyard and a Coped Stone with key patterns, beasts and knots at the ends. On a ten feet high cross in the churchyard is a primitive depiction of a man with a tail, which may have had significance in pagan fertility rites. There is also a wheel cross, simply decorated with foliage scroll.

The area to the south bears evidence of early tin streaming, where material dug out was left, to form hummocky debris on the surface. In the 1840s, Lanivet Consols and Tretoil produced thousands of tons of copper ore. Lanivet put itself on the map again in 1926 and 1927, when the Canadian and South African beam transmitters were built here. This followed Marconi's earlier experiments at Poldhu. (See Gunwalloe, Mullion, Porthcurno).

An old rhyme recalled the Lanivet Feast:

'On the nearest Sunday to the last Sunday in A-prel,
Lanivet men fare well,
On the first Sunday after the first Tuesday in May,
Lan'ivery men fare as well as they.'

Lanlivery

This village, situated above a tributary of the Fowey River, is part of a windswept, rather bleak moorland parish. It has an exceptionally fine church, whose 97 feet high tower provides a notable landmark and is considered to be one of the finest in the county.

On a wild and windy winter's night, it is not hard to understand why eerie folklore surrounds these parts. Perhaps the most chilling story is the one about the notorious Tregeagle getting drunk with the Devil here. The ballad Tregeagle, written in 1807 recounts how he sold his soul to the Devil:

'A bargaine!' A bargaine! Then said he aloude,
'At my lot I will never repyne;
I swear to observe it, I sweare by the roode,
And am readye to seale and to synge with my bloode,
Bothe my soule and my bodye are thyne!'

(see St Breock, St Teath & Lanivet).

Lanner

Lanner, a large scattered mining village to the south east of Redruth, suffered depopulation along with other mining settlements when mining was in decline in the last century, and men were forced to seek work overseas. Each week these breadwinners sent thousands of pounds home to their families, and when the South African mails arrived, people from Lanner, Portreath, Illogan, Carnkie and other local villages converged on Redruth for a mammoth spending spree. On these occasions the shops would remain open until late at night. Mr. Hosking, a miner of Lanner, who emigrated to South Africa was lucky enough to strike a 123 ounce nugget of gold, which he sent home to his wife. She deposited it in a Redruth bank for safe keeping.

Back in the 13th century,the Bishop of Exeter had enclosed the woodland of his manor here to create a deer park, but this like the other deer parks in Cornwall became neglected, and the lands were divided up and let for farming. To cast work-a-day cares aside on Boxing Day, it was traditional for crowds to assemble at the Miners' Arms for the election of the Mock Mayor. His drunken Worship, with blackened face, and wearing a big white collar, with an impressive cow chain and pendant dangling round his neck, would be hoisted onto a donkey, and paraded through the streets to the accompaniment of a fife and drum band. Returning to the rostrum to make his speech, he would drink from the Cuckle's Cup (a receptacle designed for quite another purpose). If onlookers were arrested they were subjected to various indignities. Another source of entertainment was wrestling, and in September 1860, a three hour bout between John Murton of Gwennap, and Joseph Francis of St Austell was finally brought to an end and declared a draw.

Lanreath

This quiet and attractive village off the main road to the north west of Polperro has some pleasingly grouped cottages, with an inn, a church and an Elizabethan manor house, once the home of the Grylls family. The picturesque Punch Bowl Inn is thought to date from the 13th century, while the church of St Manarck & St Dunstan has a Norman font and an Elizabethan pulpit. The Giant's Hedge, running from Lerryn to West Looe can be seen to best advantage here; its origin is obscure, but it is likely to have been an ancient fortification.

The Reverend Grylls, a rector here, once sought the assistance of the celebrated Parson Dodge in sorting out a ghostly man in black, who terrified his parishioners by driving a coach pulled by headless horses across a neighbouring moor. The pastoral pair waited patiently, but when nothing happened went home their separate ways. The strange behaviour of Parson Dodge's horse caused him to turn back, and he was horrified to see his colleague unconscious on the ground at the feet of the phantom driver. Worried villagers, who had seen their parson's horse return without him, were astonished to find him senseless in the arms of Parson Dodge. A prayer was offered, breaking the spell but not before the ghost was heard to exclaim, 'Dodge is come, I must be gone!' and evaporating into thin air. Another pastoral tale strains the credulity, for it involves an old rector, his young wife and a new curate. The inevitable happened, and shortly afterwards the old man somehow met his death at the foot of the cellar steps. A large black rook, which turned up the following day, was thought to embody the spirit of the murdered man, who had presumably returned to torment them. But the luckless ghost came to know the meaning of 'pot luck' when he inadvertantly flew in through the window of the Punch Bowl, landed in the oven, and had the door smartly closed on him by the quick thinking kitchen maid.

May Day was celebrated in these local villages by dancing around the maypole in the traditional style. If one village took too much pride in its maypole, another might make off with it. The sensible folk of Lanreath took the wise precaution of setting up guards – who steadfastly resisted dastardly attempts to get them drunk at their post (see Menheniot).

When the *Wolf Rock Lighthouse* went automatic in 1987, the *Farm and Folk Museum* here was given the old Gardener engine and the switchboard, which had done almost 30 years lighthouse service.

Lanteglos-by-Camelford, *see* **Delabole**

Latchley, *see* **Gunnislake**

Launcells

Streams and watermeadows provide a charming setting for this village just south east of Stratton, with its church, rectory, old cottages and Georgian manor house. The church, which escaped the heavy hand of the restorer, is much prized for its refreshingly light and lovely interior. Its bellringers found a place in romantic literature via

Hawker's ballard *The Ringers of Launcell's Tower*. They rang for the accession of George III in 1760, and for his jubilee. In the churchyard lies the inventive genius Sir Goldsworthy Gurney, born in 1793, a doctor who had been inspired by Trevithick's experimental work on steam locomotion. He devoted his spare time to the study of mechanical science and chemistry. Although he pioneered steam engines for use on roads, he was thwarted by legislation restricting such vehicles on highways, and so he diversified his research. His invention of the oxy-hydrogen blow pipe earned him *The Society of Art's* gold medal. As well as the Gurney Stove, he developed a high pressure steam jet used for extinguishing fires in mines and ventilating sewers. He later switched his attentions to light, and invented a kind of limelight used in lighthouse lanterns and in theatres. He spent his last years in the castle he built at Bude, situated between the river and the canal (see Marhamchurch).

Leedstown

The hamlet of Leedstown, at the junction of secondary crossroads between Hayle and Helston, is thought to have derived its name from the Duke of Leeds who acquired property here by his marriage to Mary Godolphin, daughter of Francis, the last of the male line. It was said that a young woman of Leedstown who was wooed by a false suitor for her inheritance, was tricked by him into parting with the documents, which she kept in a locked box in an upstairs room of her cottage. She went mad after he took off for America with all her wealth, and her sad and restless spirit returns to weep in a corner, or flit frantically up and down the stairs in search of her lost legacy.

Lelant

Lelant lies on the Hayle estuary and is now part of the Borough of St Ives. It was a medieval seaport, but enchroaching sand resulted in loss of trade to St Ives. In 1877 its quays were connected with the St Ives Railway by a loop line. They could accommodate ships drawing seventeen feet of water at high tide, and a new cartroad linked the village with the quay. The St Erth to St Ives branch line, which follows the coast, remains one of the most attractive scenic sections of railway in the country. Skeletons discovered during the construction of the railway through the towans add support to the theory that this was the site of the King of Cornwall's *Castle Tewdrig*. Legend has it that a whole town was lost beneath the encroaching sands in the area around the church.

Miners from here and other maritime areas frequently had shares in fishing boats, choosing to go to sea in good weather, or underground when the weather was poor. Hence the old saying:

'Get up, take breakfast, and go to the moor;
The sea tide of the morning is worth nothing.'

The church, dedicated to St Uny, an Irish saint, is perched on high ground above the mouth of the Hayle River, with sand dunes between it and the sea.

Lerryn

Approaching up the Fowey River, and veering to starboard along the course of the enchantingly beautiful Lerryn creek, one rounds a bend to behold the village described earlier this century as having 'a sweet, unspoiled atmosphere of gardens and orchards, shadowing trees and cottages embowered in blossom'. Its boats, ancient bridges, cottages, inn and chapel still help to retain its engaging old-world charm.

Fowey Regatta Day drew competitiors from Lerryn, Golant and other riverside settlements which also held regattas in their own right. The event, enthusiastically anticipated throughout the year, attracted many rowing boats from Fowey, Polruan and other places, which converged around the mudflats early in the morning, impatient for a favourable tide.

High above the west banks of the Lerryn river at *Boconnoc*, is a medieval deer park where the ancient dikes and gnarled oaks remain as a cameo of medieval landscape. Couch's Mill, delightfully set amidst the woods between Boconnoc and the village, provides another agreeable taste of bygone work-a-day charm.

Boconnoc, with its roots deep in our history, was held at the time of the Conquest by Robert de Mortain. The manor passed into the possession of the Carminow, Courtenay and Mohun families. The last Lord Mohun was an infamous duellist, killed in 1713 (see Thackeray's *Esmond*). Strangely it also had associations with another duellist, namely the second Lord Camelford, a descendant of Thomas Pitt of Madras, owner of the Pitt diamond, who acquired the estate after the Mohuns. In 1644 *Boconnoc Manor* was seized for the king, who was said to have been fired at whilst standing beneath a stout oak tree, which thereafter sprouted variegated leaves The present house dates mainly from the late 18th century. In recent years, it has become traditional for a carol service to be held in the beautiful parish church on the Boconnoc estate in aid of the Mount Edgcumbe Hospice.

The so called *Giant's Hedge*, an earthen rampart and ditch, traces of which can be seen between Lerryn and Looe, and probably a tribal boundary, was explained in folklore thus:

'One day the Devil, having nothing to do,
Built a great hedge from Lerryn to Looe.'

A variation tells us that it was Jack, the giant who had nothing to do (see Lanreath).

Linkinhorne

This slatey village to the north west of Callington has a granite church, dedicated to St Melor, with the second highest tower in Cornwall (Probus has the highest). In the churchyard, beneath the east window, is a joint tombstone bearing the inscription:

'Here we lye without the wall;
'Twas full within they made a brawl,
Here we lye no rent to pay,
And yet we lye as warm as they.'

This was the work of the 18th century philosopher, eccentric and stonecutter Daniel Gumb, who studied astronomy and *Euchlid* in his spare time, and lived the simple life in an improvised cavern fashioned from the rocks near Cheesewring, with his wife and children (see Minions). St Melor's holy well is housed in a small 15th century building, and Plusha bridge, 1½ miles to the south west, with three round headed arches, also dates from this period.

In 1879 miner William Henry Budge Seymour was found dead in his mine, supposedly as the result of a fit. After his burial a neighbour had a vivid dream about a fine gentleman turning up at his mother's house and announcing that her son had been buried alive. A group of his friends hurriedly dug him up, and reportedly found him still breathing. However, a doctor's verdict was that he had been dead for several days, and they were reprimanded for their foolishness.

Lizardtown

This long straggling village, close to Lizard Point, reflects a changing role in its mixture of old cottages and more recent development of gift shops, cafes and other needs of the present day tourist, many of which purport to be the most southerly this or that. The railway system never penetrated nearer than Helston and once it was only the well-heeled, discerning holiday maker taking excursions from resorts served by the railways who ventured this far.

The term 'The Lizard' is now loosely applied to the whole area bounded by Helston and the Helford river, although that name properly refers to the Lizard Point, which is the most southerly promontory in the British Isles. The headland, anciently known as Ocrinum, has long been a famous beacon. The present lighthouse was built in 1757 and altered in 1903.

In 1857, a fisherman risked his life by going to the aid of the ninety gun *Exmouth*, bound for Spithead, which landed in difficulties on the rocky shores to the north west of the Lizard. For this act of heroism, in which lives as well as nautical property valued at around £100,000 was saved, he was awarded the paltry sum of £5.

January 1878 initiated the sound of the Lizard foghorn with 'prolonged, reverberating echoes through the surrounding precipices and caves.' This 'very weird and melancholy' noise, together with the fascinating electric light machinery attracted numbers of sightseers. The German passenger liner *Mosel*, bound for New York, was driven ashore at Bass Point near the Lizard Signal Station in August 1882, in foggy conditions. All the passengers and much of her cargo were safely brought ashore, but the vessel was a complete wreck. Local fishermen and others who succumbed to the temptation of helping themselves to her cargo were searched and ordered to return their ill-gotten gains. However, wrecking had been a way of life along these coasts, with high ranking families including the Killigrews of Falmouth, taking the lead.

London Apprentice, *see* **Polgooth**

Longdowns, *see* **Mabe Burnthouse**

Longstone, see St Mabyn

Luckett, *see* **Stoke Climsland**

Ludgvan

This charming village with its square of stone cottages and church, lies above the east end of the fertile market garden belt, commanding glorious views of St Michael's Mount and Mount's Bay (see Gulval). At the time of Domesday, its name appeared as Ludduham.

Two distinguished sons of Cornwall have close associations with the village. The celebrated Dr William Borlase (1695-1772), antiquarian, scholar, archaeologist and naturalist, was rector here for 52 years, and is buried in the church. The church also contains monuments to the Davy family, including Sir Humphry, inventor of the miner's safety lamp and one time President of the Royal Society who was born at Varfell and spent his boyhood here. He died in Italy, but his statue graces the top of Market Jew Street in Penzance.

St Ludgvan was responsible for the miraculous springing of a well here. It was believed that no person baptised in its waters could ever be hanged, and there was stunned disbelief when a village woman met this fate: local confidence was only restored when it became established that she had actually been baptised elsewhere. Superstition was rife in these parts. During the last century a Ludgvan man who fancied that his ailing pigs had been ill-wished by his sister-in-law, beat his wife and restricted her to bread and water, on the grounds that when she reached desperation point she would be able to persuade her troublesome sister to lay off. During thunder storms Ludgvan folk opened their doors to let in the lightning, in the hope that this would bring them prosperity. They had great faith in electric storms, for it was also felt that the harvest would not ripen properly until the lightning had flashed.

Luxulyan

The small, grey village of Luxulyan, with its granite cottages and fine 15th century church, is set in farming and mining country on the edge of Bodmin Moor. In early Victorian times Joseph Thomas Treffry planned a canal and mineral railway from Par, past Ponts Mill and up the Luxulyan valley to the mining area around Bugle. The railway ascended the hill on the eastern side of the valley near Ponts Mill by a 1 in 10 incline 947 yards long, and crossed the valley on Treffry's fine granite viaduct, which is 98 feet high and 216 yards long with ten forty feet arches. It was completed in 1843, and bears the Treffry coat of arms. The incline, which came into use in 1847, was worked by water wheel at the top, and a wire rope. The station, originally known as Bridges, was re-named Luxulyan in May 1905.

Luxulyanite, distinctive of this area, is a rare and beautiful type of Cornish granite with speckled tones. It was chosen for the Duke of Wellington's sarcophagus at St. Paul's, and other prestigious schemes. A large block in a field at Trevanney was worked and polished by steam power on site, and the public was allowed to view it for a small charge before it was removed to London. In the last century John Dingle advertised locally that he was adept at cutting quality mill stones to order.

Walter Eddy, who travelled local fairs erecting swings for children piled his equipment up on his cart after a fair in Luxulyan in 1851 perched himself on top and let the horse guide him homewards to Mount Charles. He must have fallen asleep at the reins, for he was found unconscious in the road beside his upturned cart, which had been tipped over by a nearby pile of stones. After a local ox had won a prize at Bodmin Fair, folk were invited along to Luxulyan to view the happy beast grazing contentedly in its field, to place orders for its meat a couple of days later.

Castilly Henge Monument, near Lower Woon Farm, dating from Neolithic times, was adapted in the Middle Ages for the performing of religious plays.

Mabe Burnthouse

The church sits outside the village, and the flooded valleys of Falmouth's reservoir lie to the south. Local quarries were once a chief source of Cornish granite supplying stone for London's Waterloo Bridge, Chatham Docks and the harbours of Gibraltar and Singapore. Gunpowder from Kennall Gunpowder Works was used to blast an enormous block of fine grit granite out of its bed at Number 8 quarry in 1880, which was a record size from the neighbourhood at that time. Despite the industrial activity, hedgerows in the area were noted for their array of wild flowers in the last century, including the shy hairy violet and the rare creeping snapdragon.

Nearby Longdowns is the site of geothermal experiments, carried out by the Camborne School of Mining.

Madron

The village of Madron, to the north west of Penzance is of particular interest for its delightful, wide ranging views across Mount's Bay, possessing the old mother church of Penzance, its holy well and a hinterland rich in antiquities.

Looking through old books on the area, it is interesting to come across contemporary remarks about the village poor house, rated by one as 'a monstrous white erection', and described by another as having 'a dignity about its proportions and something of the quaint grace of a French chateau, that is as pleasing as it is unexpected.' Their interests were obviously architectural, rather than moral or social. The St Ives fisherman and primitive painter Alfred Wallis died here in August 1942, at the age of 87. At one time his simple, childlike paintings attracted ridicule, but painter Christopher Wood and sculptor Sven Berlin recognised his natural talent. In earlier times Captain Thomas Hocking, who felt some responsibility towards the workhouse inmates left a gift of money to provide them with an enjoyable dinner every 10th February, which was his birthday. In 1832 they were treated to a special meal to mark the coronation of King William IV. These were brutal times. The highlight of Madron Feast in 1813 was a bull-baiting match. The unfortunate beast was brought uphill three miles from Penzance, before being tethered and baited until it died (see Gulval).

St Madron's Well was arguably the most famous in Cornwall, and folk recounted many a miraculous cure; it was a kind of mini-Lourdes. Handkerchiefs and personal tokens were, and still are, suspended on nearby branches in homage to the water spirit. The lovesick dropped pins into its waters seeking portents for the future. An inspirational walk northwards across moorland leads to the intriguingly named Ding Dong Mine, possibly the oldest and most romantic in the country, and the fascinating, holed stone known as Mên-an-Tol, or the Crickstone, which was also believed to have powers of healing. Naked children suffering from rickets were passed through the hole three times against the sun, then rolled thrice in the grass, while adults with a 'kill or cure' philosophy would try to ease their backache or rheumatism by scrambling backwards and forwards through the apperture. In common with other such monuments, the Mên Scryfa, just beyond, an inscribed stone, was thought to guard a crock of gold. The whole thing collapsed and had to be re-erected after an attempt to recover the fanciful treasure.

Just to the right of the secondary road leading from Madron to Morvah, is Lanyon Quoit, a dolmen or cromlech; a huge stone on three uprights looking something like a giant milkmaid's three-legged-stool. But it is thought to be a tomb, over 3,000 years old, and formerly covered by a barrow of earth. It was once high enough for a man on horseback to ride beneath, but in 1816 it was damaged during a storm, and the uprights had to be shortened to re-erect it. Among other ancient sites in the locality are Mulfra Quoit, a partially ruined megalithic tomb, Chûn Castle, an Iron Age circular fort, Chûn Quoit, with a capstone supported by four uprights, and the Nine Maidens, the remains of a stone circle, where only six of the original stones now remain erect.

Malpas

The delightfully situated village of Malpas, close to the point where the Tresillian and Truro rivers converge, commands exquisite views of this magical haunt of herons, curlews, and modern day pleasure craft. It was formerly an important ferry crossing and busy waterway feeding Truro and Tresillian as well as being a small port in its own right. Boat building was carried out here. Cannon balls, fired in anger when Spanish ships pursued the French upriver have been found in nearby woods, and still get dredged up in fishermen's nets, along with the oysters from time to time. Romantically, this is generally acknowledged to be the land of Arthurian legend, and this the ferry crossing by which Iseult made her way across to King Mark's palace. Earlier this century a ferryboat transported animals and vehicles. Today intending passengers on the Malpas side summon the ferryman from his charming, white painted old cottage, perched on the opposite St Michael Penkevil bank by ringing the bell. If he is out of earshot it is customary for ferrywives to have their own visual system of signals such as coloured towels laid out on the rocks, to inform him of waiting passengers, who are ferried across in the 150 year old rowing boat, delightfully named *Duckweed*. This may take 10, 20, 30 minutes or so, . . .

Romantic, also, but in a bold and colourful way, are the stories concerning the big, brawny 18th century ferrywoman known to one and all as 'Jenny Mopus', capable of rowing her sturdy craft, the *Happy-go-Lucky* all the way to Falmouth or Truro. In addition to ferrying farm animals across from the Roseland side to Truro market, she provided transportation for gentry visiting Tregothnan and other local houses. She declared that the most troublesome part of her job was dealing with 'wemmin and pigs'.

Malpas, as its name implies, can be a highly dangerous place in certain weather conditions, when funnelling winds create a whirlpool effect. Twice in the last century enormous tidal waves suddenly swept upriver at low tide, and as rapidly retreated.

Manaccan

This hillside village pleasingly set in unspoilt, undulating countryside, characterised by trees, flowers and narrow lanes to the south of the Helford river, commands delightful views from the head of the enchanting Gillan Creek. The Cornish historian Richard Polwhele was once a rector here, and the church of St Manacca has long been famed for its fig tree sprouting from the south wall near the tower recalling modesty in the Garden of Eden, and offering a flavour of the Old Testament. Also with roots deep in history were the 'St George' plays enacted hereabouts, in barns, inns, fish cellars, houses or any other improvised theatre. They evolved from the old morality plays, on the theme of good triumphing over evil.

In a rather bizarre incident at the time of the Napoleonic wars, Captain Bligh, of *Bounty* fame, was arrested as a spy in the course of carrying out research for the Admiralty in the Helford River, and ordered to appear before Richard Polwhele, magistrate and vicar of Manaccan. He was thrust into the vicarage coal cellar while that gentleman finished his tea, and having been brought out, protested that he would remain silent unless granted a private consultation with the vicar. After revealing his identity and business to Polwhele, they enjoyed a sociable evening, and remained in touch for many years. Another vicar who left a mark in history was the Rev William Gregor, who discovered Gregonite (otherwise known as Manaccanite or Titanium) in the waters feeding Tregonwell Mill in 1791.

According to legend, the church of St Menaccus and St Dunstan, lying close to the Gillan Creek, some distance from its village of St Anthony-in-Meneage, was built as a thanksgiving by shipwrecked Normans. In an area of rare, engaging beauty, it faces the little village of Gillan across the creek.

Marhamchurch

The village lies on the course of the old Bude Canal, which was built in the early 1820s, to connect Launceston and Holsworthy with the port of Bude. The main cargoes were coal, slate and other building materials, as well as sand, which was used as a fertiliser on the land. Barges were employed at the seaward end, up to Helebridge, beyond which it was necessary to use tub boats, for the canal was narrow and there were six inclined planes. Stationary steam engines hauled craft from Helebridge up the first incline to Marhamchurch. But the canal was soon to lose its trade to the railway which also unfortunately proved to be short-lived.

The parish church stands beyond a wide square, flanked by thatched and slate cottages. It has a unique and interesting floor, attractively patterned by beautiful Delabole slate and finely carved bench ends. A 15th century anchoress called Cecilia Moyes dwelt in a hut attached to the north wall of the sanctuary and took part in services through a window in the wall.

'Revel Sunday', held on the Sunday following 12th August, commemorated the Feast of St Marwenna, and was followed by a secular celebration on the Monday. The elected Queen of the Revel and her attendants walked in procession to the site of St Marwenna's cell for the crowning ceremony. Father Time, wearing a flowing robe, and bearing an hour glass and scythe declared as he crowned her,

'Now look! That this by all be seen,
I here do crown thee, of this year,
The Queen!'

Then the village band headed the procession to the Revel Field, with the newly crowned Queen sitting on a white horse led by a farmer in top hat and smock.

To the north, at *Binhamy,* just outside Bude, a quadrangular moat denotes the site of a former manor house or castle, home of the eccentric Ranulph de Blanchminster, better known as 'Old Blowmanger', who effectively isolated himself by raising his drawbridge. He left most of his estate for the benefit of the poor, but was still regarded with suspicion. Hares colonising the area gave rise to the popular myth that he had returned to haunt them in animal guise.

Mawgan-in-Meneage

This village, with its delightful cottages, inn and church, in a lovely setting near the head of a creek of the Helford river, usually carries its 'Meneage' tag to distinguish it from a village of the same name in Pydar. 'Meneage' is thought to be a derivation of monk, and the 'Monks' Passage' across the nearby Helford river would seem to bear that out. The cross in the village centre has a Hiberno-Saxon inscription probably dating from the 9th or 10th century. The church, dedicated to St. Mawgan bears memorials to the wealthy and influential Vyvyan, Carminow, Reskymer and Ferrer families. The Vyvyans were one of Cornwall's richest and strongest families, and Hannibal Vyvyan, governor of St Mawes Castle, was one of Elizabeth I's most trusted men in the west.

Sir R. R. Vyvyan was a pioneering conservationist who, in 1859 appealed to local farmers to resist reaching for their shotguns when an eagle appeared in Trelowarren woods.

The old July custom of 'Leading The Furze' involved gathering and transporting bundles of furze to store as winter fuel. It was carried in ceremonial style on horseback, tethered to a pole with strong ropes, and was the cause of much celebration.

Nearby Halligye Fogou, 90 feet long and 6 feet high, excellently preserved, is the largest in Cornwall.

Mawgan Porth, *see* **St Columb Minor**

Mawnan Smith & Mawnan

This charming village, with its cottages and colourful gardens is set in an enchanting area adjacent to Falmouth Bay and the Helford River, well known for its exceptionally mild climate. The 13th century church of St Maunanus and St Stephen at Mawnan about a mile and a half to the south east, enjoys an idyllic, clifftop setting above Parson's Beach. From these cliffs there have been a number of sightings of the local sea monster, a dinosaur-like creature with a long neck, small head and hump, and known as *Morgawr* (see Portscatho).

Medrose, *see* **Delabore**

Menheniot

The old routes converging on Menheniot, a pleasingly placed village above the Seaton valley, bear witness to its importance as a rural centre in the past. Today it is close to the modern A38 and the mainline railway. Slate quarrying throughout Cornwall is of very ancient origin, and the slate of Menheniot had the distinction of being described as the best in the county in the 15th century.

A rail accident at Menheniot in December 1873, caused by the confusion of two railwaymen being called 'Richard', brought about the introduction of starting signals. The signal porter's 'Right away, Dick!' prompted two goods trains waiting in the station for their 'line clear' order to pull out in opposite directions. The up-train then collided with another goods train on a bend in a cutting, half way to St Germans, killing one driver, badly injuring the other and damaging both locomotives. Another disaster occurred in 1897, when girders were being placed on the new viaduct at Coldrennick, by a gang of men working from a platform 130 feet above ground. As the platform tipped, Samuel Stephens managed to grab a cross trestle, hanging precariously suspended until rescued by workmates, but the other twelve men were hurled into the ravine below. Nine were buried in Menheniot churchyard, the other three at Liskeard.

The church, dedicated to St Lalluwy, and one of Cornwall's spired churches is thought to be where the famous Bishop Trelawny was baptised. Poole Court, a former mansion of the Trelawny's served as a poorhouse for many years. The Trelawnys of nearby Coldrennick, also included among their number, Captain E. J. Trelawny, who took part in the Greek Freedom struggle of 1824/25, who planted the rare conifers, and who was a great friend of the poets Shelley and Byron. Sir William Trelawny was a sportsman and gentleman of whom it was said, 'a better one never threw a leg over a horse.'

Menheniot's races, held on a course at Higher Click Tor Farm, were well supported in the last century. May Day was another highlight of the year, where rivalry developed between the villages in a bid to create the most spectacular, garlanded maypoles. This led to the playful custom of making off with other folk's maypoles, which led to inventing a new supersitition about bad luck descending on those who failed to return 'borrowed' maypoles before the great event. To avoid all this, it was prudent to guard the maypole some days in advance, or to cement it into position (see Lanreath).

Mevagissey

Mevagissey, with its inner and outer harbour alive with colourful fishing boats, winding streets, alleyways and quaint, picturesque cottages striding up the hillsides, still retains much of its engaging old world charm, despite the pressures of modern tourism. The oldest part of the town was named Porthilly, indicating a saltwater cove or harbour. These cottages, specially designed for the drying and mending of nets, were built to a deep plan, with a central door. Mevagissey fisherfolk described the movement of washing being dried by the cottage fires as 'John Liddicoat's Cobwebs', and believed them to be capable of foretelling a gale. The distinctive Watchman's House, built into the rock on the harbour was used in the filming of *Johnny Frenchman*.

In days of yore, huge quantities of pilchards were brought in by the Mevagissey fishing fleet, 'cured' in rock salt, packed in casks and exported to Italy and the West Indies. Some were compressed to obtain lamp oil for local use. The navy, which received supplies of this savoury fish nicknamed it the 'Mevagissey Duck'. Small pilchards came to be known as sardines in Cornwall, and in the early 1870s, about 10,000 tons of sardines per week were being produced at the factory. But in 1876 a shortage of fish led to loss of work. Mevagissey folk's ability to adapt led to a switch from seine fishing to the use of drift nets. Another innovation was brought about by the use of the steam tug *Petrel*, engaged on pier construction in 1894, which towed the fishing boats out to their fishing grounds in calm weather, allowing them to return laden the following morning.

Sharp eyed fisherman Matthias Dunn spotted a small boat about five miles to the north of Eddystone in 1857, and going to its assistance found the crew of the *Edward*, which had sunk after leaving Penryn bound for Plymouth with a cargo of cut granite. They had managed to leap into the ship's boat which was being towed astern as the vessel rolled over. He landed them at Plymouth, having lost all their possessions, but thankful to be alive. Another victim of shipwreck, which met with a less happy fate, was a monkey, washed ashore from a doomed French ship. The fisherman who found it, promptly hanged it, fearing it might be a spy.

Mevagissey was seriously affected by the cholera epidemic of 1849. About half the population sought refuge in Port Mellon, while their houses were fumigated. There were suspicions that the dreaded disease might be associated with fish in some way, so the village suffered from the decline of its livelihood as well as the deaths of the victims. A sad incident at this time concerned a fishing boat from Mevagissey, which surruptiously landed a sick man on Fowey Quay, then rapidly disappeared. No one would take him in at Fowey, as he was from Mevagissey, but they hit on the idea of isolating him in a boat out on the water, watched over at a safe distance by another boat. He died soon afterwards and was sent to Mevagissey for interment. When the Mevagissey boat emerged from its hiding place upriver, it was ordered off at gunpoint.

With the building up of hostility against Russia, six Mevagissey coastguards were sent to join the Baltic Fleet. But apparently the good folk of 'Mevva' had not heard that old adadge about not counting one's chicks, for an inaccurate rumour about the fall of Sebastopol in October 1854 caused them to go ahead with victory celebrations, creating an effigy of the Czar Nicholas to be burnt on an enormous bonfire along with the ceremonial blazing of tar barrels, traditional in Cornwall. Despite discovering the truth, they were in a mood for celebration so the effigy was carried through the streets as planned (see Goldsithney).

Nearby Bodrugan's Leap recalls the War of the Roses, when Sir Henry Bodrugan, a supporter of the House of York, leapt from the cliffs into a boat bound for France, hotly pursued by the Lancastrians. When the boat was a safe distance from the shore, he paused and roundly cursed the Trevanion and Edgcumbe families. A Bodrugan farm is the last to have ploughed with oxen.

Port Mellon, over the hill from Mevagissey, with a handful of cottages and buildings at the head of a small creek always had a touch of 'class' about it, attracting immaculately dressed 'yachty' types. The craft of boatbuilding has long been traditional at Port Mellon and Mevagissey.

Old Watchouse, Mevagissey

Michaelstow

Michaelstow is one of a string of attractive, lesser known small villages along the valley of the Camel, on the western side of Bodmin Moor. Its church of St Michael enjoys a particularly lovely setting by a green, with a fine old cross, a holy well and the remains of a hermit's cell.

Helsbury, just to the north is a circular hill fort with a single rampart and ditch. The hilltop was later the site of St Syth's chapel.

Millook, *see* Jacobstow

Minions

This moorland village to the north of Liskeard lies in a harsh rolling landscape, rich in prehistory. There was no settlement here before the mineral railway first traversed the area, and the place derives its name from the nearby tumulus known as Minions Mound. It has associations in the satisfying 'rags to riches' tradition, for in 1836 a group of working miners made their fortunes by discovering copper in Caradon Hill which is capped by a tumulus and now by a TV station. Many of Liskeard's fine buildings were financed by 'copper money'. The Cheesewring Hotel at Minions built in 1874 as a private residence claims the distinction of being the county's highest above sea level.

Construction of a railway line, planned to link the Caradon mines, Cheesewring and Tokenbury to the Liskeard Canal, started in 1844, and half a mile of track on granite blocks was soon completed and fenced. In November the railway was opened as far as Tremabe, with important folk 'partaking of dejeuner', and mere workmen enjoying good old 'roast beef and strong beer'. But transporting the ores three miles by railway and another three miles by cart to the canal was not without difficulty and many preferred to load up the horse-drawn carts at the mine to be taken direct to the canal.

The Liskeard and Caradon horse-drawn railway opened in 1846. It was skilfully engineered with cuttings and gradients, so that traffic could run by gravity all the way down to Moorswater. Down gradient traffic operated in the afternoons and evenings, controlled by brakesmen, and the empty waggon train was hauled back next morning by hired horses. In 1856 the *Cheesewring Granite Company* leased the Kilmar

Granite sent from the Duchy, and a railway opening in 1858 met with the Cheesewring branch at Minions. The cheesewring from which the place took its name is situated on Stowe's Hill. A cheesewring is an intriguing formation of flattish, weathered boulders, with large stones poised in a rather unlikely manner on smaller ones.

The notable 18th century stonecutting philosopher Daniel Gumb and his family chose to live the simple, contemplative life in a humble shelter near the railway track, constructed of thumbled boulders (see Linkinhorne). Half a mile to the north of Minions is Rillaton Round Barrow, where a bronze dagger and golden beaker were found, which bore a resemblance to those of Mycenaean Greece.

Cheesewring, Bodmin Moor

Mitchell, *see* **Summercourt**

Mithian, *see* **St Agnes**

Moorswater

The story of Moorswater reads like the story of local transport systems over the last 150 years. The *Liskeard and Looe Union Canal,* part of which started operating in 1827, ran up to Moorswater, while the road from Moorswater to Liskeard at Dean Well was constructed in 1829. This was disliked by the Trustees of the Liskeard Turnpike, for it led to a loss in revenue. The road became part of the A38 into Liskeard, which has more recently been superceded by the by-pass.

Once Moorswater became the head of navigation it usurped the traditional trade that gave neighbouring Sandplace its name. Other cargoes included coal, metal ores, manure, grain, bricks, timber, limestone, burnt lime, hay, straw and salt. Several limekilns were built here and at other points along the way, again, siphoning trade from Sandplace. Barges brought limestone around from the Plymouth quarries. In 1849 it was taking eight hours for the seven mile journey up from Looe harbour, where twenty four locks had to be negotiated. Thirteen boats with capacities of sixteen tons were operating, and there were complaints that quantities of ore were getting washed away whilst it sat on Moorswater quays awaiting transhipment.

The railway opened in 1860, and trade on the canal declined as it became increasingly choked up, and it finally ceased functioning around 1909. A mineral railway from the Caradon mines to Moorswater opened in 1846 (see Minions). The Looe line was opened to passengers in 1879. The rebuilding of the Moorswater viaduct gave a boost to the flagging granite industry. Moorswater was thus the upper terminus of the canal and the Looe railway, and the lower terminus for the Caradon railway. Most of the old station buildings and other relics of fascinating industrial archaeology were lost in the course of road widening, the by-pass and the development of the industrial estate. The old reservoir has been built over, and little trace remains of the interesting, but short-lived canal project.

Viaduct at Moorswater

Morvah

Morvah is situated in an old mining area near the wild and spectacular north coast between Zennor and Pendeen, which is exceptionally rich in sites of archaeological interest, such as Chûn Quoit, Chûn Castle, Lanyon Quoit and Gurnards Head Promontory Fort, one mile north of Porthmeor. Chûn Castle is of particular significance as a habitated fort, with surviving hut circles and stone walls (see Madron). The area had close links from early times with Brittany and Ireland, and Irish gold bracelets from the Bronze Age were discovered here. Its unusual name has been linked with the Breton 'morverch', giving rise to romantic associations with mermaids. Other subscribe to the theory of Morvah indicating 'locus maritimus'.

Another legendary association, albeit somewhat less dainty, was the giant Holiburn, said to have killed a local lad with a friendly, playful tap on the head, and pined to death in remorse. Others argue that he was wholly bad; the sort of giant who needed a diminutive figure to put him in his rightful place. Artful Jack the Tinner aptly fitted the bill – by luring him into a pit by the church and covering him with stones. Some say the giant's protests can still be heard beneath the stone known as the Giant's Grave. Both theories credited him with the creation of Morvah Feast, which drew such large and enthusiastic crowds on the nearest Sunday to the first day in August, that it gave rise to the old proverb, 'Three on one horse – like going to Morvah Fair!' Wrestling and quoit throwing were particularly popular activities.

A strange old custom of Morvah decreed that the families and friends of newly weds might pull them from their bed, beat them with a sand filled sack, place prickly furze on their palliasse, then leave them to their own devices.

Morwenstow

The village of Morwenstow lies in a secluded combe on the spectacular coast north of Bude, in a sparsely populated area, characterised by rolling farmland, isolated farmsteads and small, scattered settlements. Its name is Celtic, with the additional Saxon 'Stow'. The church of St Morwenna is of ancient foundation, and is reckoned to be one of the county's most interesting. It has some particularly fine examples of Norman architecture.

Morwenstow is popularly associated with the eccentric parson and poet Robert Stephen Hawker, who spent childhood holidays in Stratton and developed a deep love of the area. This remarkable, temperamental, neurotic, whimsical, impulsive, compassionate, courageous and dutiful man, who tended to go from one extreme to another, born in Plymouth in 1803, was vicar here from 1834 to 1875, married a Bude woman twice his age, then having been widowed after nearly forty years, married a Polish governess forty years his junior, and became a father. He was a controversial figure, much loved and also despised, and became a Roman Catholic on his deathbed.

Hawker restored the church, built the vicarage and constructed a timber hut from material found on the beach and hauled up the cliff. This is where he is thought to have written *The Quest of the Sangraal*, published in 1863. However, his best known work is *The Song of the Western Men*, which he tried to pass off as an authentic ballad he had come across by chance. This rousing song, incorporating those immortal lines 'And shall Trelawny die . . . Here's twenty thousand Cornishmen shall know the reason why . . .' has become accepted as Cornwall's National Anthem, recalling Bishop Trelawny's refusal to sign the Declaration of Indulgence, and his being brought to trial by James II, thereby making him a folk hero among the independently minded Cornish.

Parson Hawker wrote of the area which had long been notorious for its grim record of shipwrecks:

'From Padstow Point to Lundy Light,
Is a watery grave both day and night.'

He was very concerned about shipwreck, with its tragic loss of life, and the dignity such victims might be entitled to in death (see St Gennys & Gunwalloe). Not surprisingly, the churchyard is the last resting place for many who met that fate. His humanitarian teachings had a great impact on some of his unlikely parishioners, who included in their number many hard-nosed smugglers, wreckers and other dubious characters. He was an author and poet of some repute, but tended to colour up situations and focus dimly recalled legends into prominence. He liked to play practical jokes on people, and once masqueraded as a seaweed clad mermaid, sitting on a rock singing falsetto in the moonlight. When fully clothed he favoured fishermen's jerseys, long sea boots and flamboyant purple clothes worn to attract attention. He is now perhaps best remembered for reviving the Harvest Festival Service, now celebrated in churches all over the world.

The Composite Signals Organisation have established a satellite station here, thereby carrying on Cornwall's traditional key role in worldwide communications (see Gunwalloe, Porthcurno & Lanivet).

Mousehole

As dawn broke on 23rd July 1595, the strengthening sunlight began to disperse a thick sea mist over Mount's Bay, eerily revealing the awesome sight of three Spanish galleys riding at anchor off St Clement's Isle. The panic-stricken villagers took to their heels as armed soldiers came ashore in small boats, and proceeded to sack and plunder. The story goes that Jenkin Keigwin was struck by a cannon ball as he bravely tried to defend his home, now the oldest remaining building in the village, known as the Keigwin Arms. The marauding Spaniards rushed on up the hill, turning their attentions to the village of Paul and its church, before creating devastation in Newlyn and

Penzance. They met with scant resistance until Sir Francis Godolphin rallied the local men, and sent for re-inforcements.

Colonies of Spaniards settled around Mount's Bay (as they did around Tor Bay), particularly at Mousehole, where, in the last century, it was reported that they could be distinguished by their Andalusian features. They came at various times over the last three hundred years, particularly after the defeat of the Armada.

Mousehole was one of the last strongholds of the Cornish language, and was the home of Dolly Pentreath, who has gone down in popular folk history as being the last person to speak the Cornish language (see Paul & Zennor). This claim has beeen contested. Some say she was an artful old woman, who persistently begged, and would oblige people by jabbering in Cornish if the price was right, or would curse them for nothing if it was not. Merlin's Rock at Mousehole is claimed to be the place where King Arthur dined after being summoned to repel an invasion, but Sennen's 'Merlin's Rock' is similarly linked with Arthurian legend. Folklore also surrounds the well known cave, avoided at night for fear of being lured inside by that dastardly Dicky Danjy. But caves such as this played their role in the flourishing smuggling industry, and this may have originated from a tale prudently put about by those involved in it. Smuggling was an accepted way of life in these parts, as illustrated in 1771, when Richard Pentreath was described by Penzance's Collector of Customs as being 'an honest man in all his dealings, though a notorious smuggler.' Mousehole folk had a reputation for hard drinking, until John Wesley preached them out of it.

The place, originally known as Porth Enys, the 'island port' (referring to St Clement's Isle), was of early importance, and has always been dependant on fishing. Pilchards were cured here, but the remainder of the catch was taken into Newlyn, allowing Mousehole to remain a quiet haven, with its compact little harbour, picturesque fishermen's cottages imaginatively placed along steep and twisting narrow lanes, which once glistened with pilchard scales in the season. The inhabitants were poor; fish and vegetables formed their staple diet, and meat was scarce. Until recent times, Mousehole was a work-a-day place with a strong smell of fish, which tended to hasten travellers on their way. In addition to this, neatly walled front gardens formerly contained manure heaps, popular with the fowl and pigs, rather than flowers.

Almost anything was considered suitable to be placed in a pie, and nothing was wasted. Hence the tradition of putting whole pilchards in pies, with heads uppermost, gazing at the sky, aptly becoming known as Starry Gazy Pie. Tom Bawcock's Eve, celebrated on 23rd December, recalls the occasion he put to sea and caught enough fish to satisfy the starving villagers, for:

'A merry place you may believe,
Was Mouzel on Tom Bawcock's Eve,
To be there then who wudn' wish
To sup on sebn sorts o' fesh.'

It is poignant to reflect that villlagers were eagerly preparing for this festival in 1981 when the entire crew of the lifeboat *Solomon Browne*, the cream of their manhood, was lost going to the aid of the *Union Star*, and became immortalised as heroes of the sea. The Penlee lifeboat has taken part in many daring incidents in these notoriously dangerous waters. In 1947 the *W & S* lifeboat rescued all eight members of *H.M.S. Warspite*, which had become stranded on Mount Malpas Ledge in Mount's Bay, and Coxswain Edward M. Madron was awarded the Silver Medal and the Maud Smith award for the bravest lifeboat deed of the year.

The Mousehole Wild Bird Hospital & Sanctuary, now run by the R.S.P.C.A., was founded by Dorothy and Phyllis Yglesias, who moved here in 1925. Dylan Thomas and his wife Caitlin spent their honeymoon here, after being married at Penzance Registry Office in 1937, and were much influenced by the place and its characters, while artist Christopher Wood and a host of others found creative inspiration here.

Mullion

Mullion, on the west coast of the Lizard peninsula, was originally a little fishing settlement and a notorious haunt of smugglers and wreckers. It must have been a magnificent sight in November 1860, when a large fleet of over two hundred sailing vessels, which had been sheltering from a violent storm in Mullion Roads and Porthleven Bay, simultaneously set sail in the calm that followed. Strong east winds in April 1897 again caused shipping to seek shelter in Mullion Roads, and fishermen from all over the Lizard lost most of their gear. Local folk helped out by cutting withies from the hedgerows to create a new supply of vital crabpots, necessary for their livelihood and food supplies.

Many other vessels have come to grief along this section of coast. In March 1867 the *Jonkeer*, homeward bound from the East Indies with a cargo of spices, sugar, coffee and a quantity of tin, broke her back on the rocks of Mên-y-Grib during a terrific storm. Of the 26 on board only a Greek crewman survived. The captain's body was never found, but his mistress and their baby born during the voyage, and other drowned victims were laid out on the shore, before being taken for burial in the churchyard.

Towards the end of the last century the fast moving world of technology and communications began to catch up with this once remote area. In 1880, the mail was brought to Mullion and the surrounding villages by cart from Helston, rather than on foot, and it was timed to co-incide with the London trains. Well-heeled holidaymakers began to arrive who regarded the local way of life, the boats and the scenery as quaint and recreational. Local folk, somewhat bemused by the intruders saw a new means of livelihood opening up for them, and many of the houses began to take in visitors. Nearby Poldhu became world famous as the site for the Marconi Wireless Telegraphy Station, from which Marconi, in Newfoundland, received the first Morse signal transmitted across the Atlantic from here on 12 December, 1901.

Mullion was physically placed more firmly on the map when solid tyred GWR buses linked it with Helston Station in 1903. Again, the area found itself in the forefront of progress when the first single flight of an airship from Mullion Air Station was made in June 1916. Mullion Airfield was also operational in the last war.

The area around Mullion Cove, more correctly known as Porth Mellin, is now in the care of the National Trust, while the island, whimsically thought to resemble a lion couchant, is managed by Cornwall Naturalists' Trust.

Mylor Churchtown & Mylor Bridge

Mylor, like other Celtic settlements of the Fal estuary, provided excellent facilities for navigation, with the advantage of being concealed within the haven and therefore less vulnerable to seaward attack. Mylor Churchtown is situated where the creek opens out into the main estuary, with its church occupying a particularly enchanting situation near the water. In Cornwall a churchtown is a settlement around the old church usually very small and not to be confused with a town. This church, dedicated to St Melorus, has two Norman doorways and a particularly fascinating churchyard containing the graves of many shipwrecked victims, a detached bell tower and Cornwall's tallest cross, measuring seventeen feet six inches in full. This was discovered, base uppermost, acting as a south wall buttress in 1870, and some of its height had been sacrificed in the course of re-erecting it.

The shipwright, Joseph Crapp, who died as the result of an accident in 1770 at the age of 43, was not allowed to slip into obscurity, for his tombstone captures the imagination for posterity, by letting us in on the knowledge that:

> 'His foot, it slip,
> And he did fall,
> Help, help, he cries,
> And that was all.'

Another tombstone tells of the tragic fate that awaited young Thomas James at the hands of a customs officer as he returned from a fishing trip:

> 'Officious zeal in luckless hour laid wait,
> And wilful sent the murderous ball of fate!
> James to his home, which late in health he left,
> Wounded returns – of life is soon bereft.'

Mylor's former diminutive Royal Naval Dockyard had the distinction of being the smallest in the world. In the 1830s it was a dockyard with an established cooperage and a store for shot, with the frigate *Astraea* anchored in Carrick Roads serving as a storeship and general headquarters. When Falmouth's *Post Office Packet Service* came under the jurisdiction of the Admiralty, it was decided in 1835 that the old brigs of war which replaced the packets should come here for repair, instead of Plymouth. After the bulk of the mail trade was taken over by Southampton, the frigate remained in a caretaking capacity. The place was revived in 1854 for the repairing of government ships.

A nearby headland, known as Tarra Point, derived from the Cornish word for 'bull', recalls the day early in the last century when a terrifying black bull, which nobody could account for, suddenly appeared, rushed madly through the streets breathing fire and roaring, then as suddenly, vanished. A more rational, and annual event was the calculated farce associated with the electing of the mock mayor. The journeymen tailors, decked out in colourful finery would elevate one of their number to this dubious position, in a loud ceremony, characterised by humbug and disrespect, before carting their new mayor back to Penryn, for more serious drinking, more silly speeches and a spectacular climax with blazing bonfires and fireworks.

Mylor Bridge, situated at the head of the creek, with its engaging, mellow charm has proved a happy environment for writers. Katherine Mansfield and John Middleton Murry took a cottage here, which had a garden running down to the water's edge. They came here after leaving D. H. Lawrence and Frieda at Zennor. Katherine frequently visited London and other places, while Murry spent much of his time alone. Howard Spring, whose ashes were laid in the churchyard, came to live in 1939 in a bungalow on Hooper's Hill, with a fine view down the creek.

To the north east of Mylor Bridge is the hauntingly beautiful Restronguet Creek, once busy with oyster dredgers, Truro river barges and vessels making for port of Devoran. At the foot of the steep hill is the charming thatched Pandora Inn, looking like something that escaped from the pages of a favourite storybook. It was once owned by Captain Edwards, who sailed out to the South Seas to bring the mutineers aboard the *Bounty* to justice. He renamed the inn, which was formerly known as the Ship Inn, after his own ship, which was wrecked after capturing Captain Bligh's mutineers.

Pandora Inn, Restronguet

Nancekuke, *see* Perranwell

Nanpean

Around Nanpean, and the area to the west of St Austell, the granite is in the form of china stone, important industrially after grinding down, as it forms the base for the manufacture of porcelain. This large, industrial village with its terraced houses lies in a landscape blown through with white dust, with a stark, brooding beauty all of its own. In recent years the dust has been reduced and the clay overburdens, topped and landscaped. The place retains its vigorous identity, far removed from 'touristy' images of Cornwall.

Following the construction of the Hendra Down – Newquay Harbour railway in 1849, there were plans to link Burngullow with the St Dennis branch of the Newquay Railway, near the village of Hendra. However, only three miles of single line track from Burngullow to the Drinnick Mill Clay Works near Nanpean were constructed before the money ran out. This three mile section opened in 1869, for mineral traffic, using the secondhand broad gauge locomotives *Newquay* and *Phoenix*. As the result of a legal dispute, there was ¾ mile 'break' in the line at Carpella from December 1909 to 18th April 1922, when it was restored.

Longstone Downs to the east evokes the legend of a giant who lost his hat to a gust of wind and thrust his staff into the ground while trying to catch it – only to lose both. Passers by found his hat, which they took to be a millstone, and his staff, which was on the scale of a longstone, and the name stuck.

Newlyn Harbour

Newlyn

Newlyn, with its busy and colourful harbour, narrow streets, delightful fishermen's cottages, courts and alleyways and penetrating bright light, retains much of the character and charm which attracted artists there towards the end of the last century. These artists, who had been influenced by the French Impressionists came to be known collectively as the Newlyn School. Today Newlyn has the style and dignity of a thriving, modern fishing port, with boats from all over the world. It is interesting at any time, particularly early in the morning when the fish market is in action. Old guidebooks enthused more over the evenings: 'The sun has sunk behind the western hills. The little town and its fishing fleet are in shadow, but a shaft of bright light is illuminating the topsails of a schooner and transmitting the long line of the outer quay into a great bar of gold. In the distance Penzance is similarly transfigured; while across the bay St Michael's Mount glows like the inspired frontispiece to some poet's dream.'

Newlyn fishermen were reputedly the last in this area to observe the age old custom of throwing fish into the ocean as a thanks-offering to the sea spirits. At various times, such as in 1830, when the fisheries failed, fishermen and their families became virtually destitute. So the paying of church tithes, considered unjustified and outmoded, was much resented, as a solicitor and bailiff who visited Mousehole and Newlyn found to their cost, having been set upon by the womenfolk of the two villages. The area gave rise to spirited women, amongst them the octogenarian fishwife Mary Kelynack, who walked all the way to London in her working garb to make a point about her pension rights. In doing so, she touched the heart of Queen Victoria, attracted the attention of the press and became the darling of the smart set.

The folk of Newlyn also demonstrated their ability to put up a fight, and attract the attention of the media in 1937, when bureaucratic vandalism, in the guise of 'slum clearance', threatened their much cherished homes with demolition. A deputation of Newlyners set off in the long liner *Rosebud*, and sailed right up the Thames to the Houses of Parliament to put their case. This spirited send-off recalls the departure of the local built fishing lugger *Mystery* in 1854, when seven enterprising young fishermen set off for Australia, lured by the adventure and romance of the gold rush. A model of the vessel was used as a centrepiece of a Cornish display as part of Australia's Bicentenary Celebrations in 1988, while at Newlyn a plaque commemorates the epic voyage.

At the end of Newlyn's South Pier, close to the lighthouse is the Tidal Observatory, which has been supplying the Ordnance Survey with data since 1915. The place is of worldwide importance, keeping records of mean sea levels, baragraph readings, sea temperatures and climate. There was an appalling incident at the lighthouse in 1896, when the keeper went to extinguish the light in the top section and found the whole lot ablaze. He turned off the oil supply, but the heat melted the equipment, causing it to burst and shower him with oil. He was unable to escape from the trapdoor, and the increasing heat caused the windows to shatter, so in desperation he managed to get outside the gallery at the top of the structure, and scream for help. Some workmen on the pier managed to rescue him with ropes and get him home, where his burns were dressed by the Newlyn nurse.

Newlyn East

The quiet village of Newlyn East lies at the centre of a spider's web pattern of narrow, winding lanes on a high ridge. It commands impressive views over china clay country, and to the Atlantic between Trevose Head and St Agnes Beacon. It is close to the course of the now disused railway line, running from Newquay through the charmingly named Fiddler's Green, to Perranporth, St Agnes and Chacewater, where it converged with the main line. During the last century, this was Cornwall's main lead mining area. East Wheal Rose Mine, on Newlyn Downs, was the scene of Cornwall's worst mining disaster when in 1846, a freak storm flooded the mine, and 39 men were drowned. A disused stone quarry was fashioned around that time, to create a Methodist venue in the style of John Wesley's Gwennap Pit. Religion was well represented in the village, for there were Methodist chapels, one Gothic, the other Georgian, as well as a church dedicated to St Newlina.

Legend would have us believe that Newlina, an Irish maiden fled here to escape the amorous attentions of a pagan prince, that he followed, and that she literally lost her head when she refused to marry him. To add good measure a spring erupted where her head hit the ground. Before her death the maiden emplanted her staff near the church, where a fig tree flourished. It was said that anyone attempting to pluck the fruit or leaves would swiftly be struck down.

Trerice, just to the north, was for centuries the seat of the Arundell family, whose most illustrious member was the brave Colonel John Arundell, who stoutly defended Pendennis Castle during the Civil War. This fine Elizabethan manor house is now in the care of the National Trust.

New Mill, *see* **Zennor**

North Hill

This pleasant, unspoilt village on the north eastern edge of Bodmin Moor lies in a steep, remote area, close to the River Lynher, with valleys, tors, wooded slopes, and farming country to the east. Across the Lynher are the rocky eminences of Hawk's Tor and Twelve Men's Moor. The latter derives it name from the lease granted in 1284 to twelve local men by the Prior of Launceston. Stone used in the construction of Westminster Bridge was quarried nearby.

The village has a Methodist chapel, a large, decorated, mainly 15th century church, with many interesting monuments, including some to the Trebartha family, some lovely old manor buildings and some slate and slate-hung cottages. The Race Horse Inn was formerly a schoolroom. Berriow Bridge, to the south, dates from medieval times. It is said that Vincent Darley, who died in 1764, and lived at Battens farmhouse returns to haunt the area in three guises. Sometimes he walks home from Darley Ford with a bundle of sticks, sometimes he returns to drive his coach recklessly around the farmyard, and occasionally turns up in the form of a black dog.

Otterham

Otterham is tranquil these days, but the surrounding tumuli and earthworks bear witness to its original importance. At the time of Domesday, this area between Camelford and Stratton was a manor known as Othram. Otterham Mill was built to harness the waters of a tributary of the Ottery River, which makes its course eastwards to join the Tamar near Launceston. The course of the now disused railway line, linking Launceston with Wadebridge runs nearby. The tiny village in its treeless, boggy and rather desolate environment, has a church with a low tower by a Tudor farm, approached down a lane, and a network of paths linking it with outlying settlements.

Pantersbridge, *see* **Warleggan**

Par

Ports accessible to the china clay areas around St Austell developed in the 19th century, beginning with Charlestown in 1800, Pentewan in 1826, Par harbour in 1828, then Fowey in 1869. Par and Fowey were destined to become the two major outlets in the latter part of the century. Par harbour was constructed on reclaimed land by the famous engineer, J. T. Treffry, who also built the fine viaduct at Luxulyan. In early Victorian times, Treffry had a vision of creating a canal from Par harbour to Ponts Mill, to link with the mineral railway up the Luxulyan valley to the moorland area of Molinnis. The whole system, with the viaduct and incline came into use in 1847.

The factories, chimneys and buildings were once coated with powdery white dust, exuding an almost surrealist charm, but efforts have been made to reduce this in recent years. A lead smelting works was built in the 1840s, with an excessively tall stack to carry away the fumes, and another one was built in 1865. They soon found a niche in local folklore. Gentlemen sporting stylish 'belltoppers' were not at all amused when cheeky folk called out 'Par stack!' as they swept by.

Par's lovely stretch of sands and the coming of the railway put it on the tourist map. In 1861 the countryside between here and Lostwithiel was lit up when a truckload of hay on a goods train caught alight in the tunnel and threatened to set fire to the station. Fortunately a quick thinking engineer detached the truck, passed it under the water tank, and effectively quenched it. Eleven years later a near head-on collision of trains on the single track of the Cornwall Railway, when a china clay train overshot St Austell Station and careered on down the gradient towards a mail train coming up from Par, was narrowly averted by the quick thinking driver of the mail train, who slammed his engine into reverse and shot backwards at full speed, chased by the speeding down train. A narrow gap remained between them as they both came to a halt at the station, while the distressed and shocked passengers plied the hero with gifts.

On St Nicholas Day, it was customary for the choirboys of Par to elect one of their number Boy Bishop, to dress in fine robes and lead the hymn singing.

Paul

The village and churchtown of Paul, on a hill above Mousehole, although small, is remarkable for the people connected with it, some of whom are buried here. The church, whose lofty tower is a well known landmark, was burnt down by the Spaniards in 1595 and took another battering in 1942. The Cornish epitaph of 1709 to Captain Stephen Hutchens, who left a bequest for the church and for the founding of the almshouses, can be translated as:

'Eternal life be his whose loving care,
Gave Paul an almshouse and the church repair.'

This inscribed stone is claimed to be the only survivor of its kind left in Cornwall.

Penzance, which had become a fashionable watering place at the time of the Napoleonic wars attracted visiting royalty and the gentry to the area, some of whom settled in stylish residences. Thus Paul churchtown was visited by Prince Louis Lucien Bonaparte and also by Prince Felix Youssoupoff, who played a major role in the political assasination of the mad monk Rasputin in St Petersburgh in 1916. The antiquarian linguist Prince Louis Lucien Bonaparte sponsored the inscribed stone to Dolly Pentreath, now emplaced in the churchyard wall, and giving credence to her claim to have been the last person to speak the Cornish language. The inscription begins: 'Here lieth interred Dorothy Pentreath, who died in 1777 said to have been the last person who conversed in the ancient Cornish, the peculiar language of this county from the earliest records, till it expired in the 18th century in this parish of St. Paul. . .'

William Bodenor of Mousehole is also buried in this churchyard and cited as a later speaker of Cornish, while John Davey of Boswednack near Zennor (1812-92) is another rival claimant.

More recently, in 1955, Lamorna Birch, one of the Newlyn School of painters who lived at Lamorna, was buried here, with his wife Emily Houghton, while members of the Yglesias family also lie in the churchyard. The sisters Dorothy and Phyllis (Pog), founded the Wild Bird Hospital and Sanctuary at Mousehole in 1928 (see Mousehole).

Local folk were particularly concerned about the weather on the feast day of St Pol de Lion, which fell on the Sunday nearest to October 10th, for the old proverb warned, 'Rain for Paul, rain for all,' predicting a wet twelve months. On Feasten Monday it was traditional for Paul men to play an annual bowling match with Mousehole men, an event sedately celebrated in Victorian times with church or chapel teas, and concerts in the schoolroom.

Pelynt

Pelynt lies to the north of Polperro and is a small village with a medieval church and wishing well. Trelawne House to the south east, originated in the 13th century, but reflects the work of several centuries. It was the home of Sir Jonathan Trelawny, who came here from Alternun in 1600, bringing the name of his former estate with him. Some believe him to have been Bishop Trelawny, of the famed *And shall Trelawny die?* (see Morwenstow). Others maintain that it was more likely to have been Sir John Trelawny, leader of the King's party under James I, and committed to the Tower in 1627.

Penberth, *see* **Porthcurno**

Pendeen

From Pendeen to Cape Cornwall, the greenstone, which is even more resistant to erosion than granite, gives rise to high inaccessible cliffs, and windswept trees bent by the bracing Atlantic breezes. The village of Pendeen, for long a prosperous centre of tin mining, has also known hard times brought about by the vagaries of the tin market. Their church of St John was built by unemployed tin miners in 1851.

In more recent times, Geevor mine incorporated part of the old Levant mine, with one gallery 2,000 feet below the seabed, and another extending a mile offshore. In 1850, tin miners of Levant, who were working on the beach, were picked up by a wave, dragged out to sea and never seen again. Their shirts were later found near Pendeen. Some outbreaks of typhoid fever were attributed to contaminated water from an adit (horizontal entrance) under the man-engine, and this pinpointed the need for fresh water to be taken into the mines for drinking purposes. The well known Levant mine provided the training ground for many of the foremost mining men, who went on to work in mines all over the world.

Pendeen House was the birthplace of William Borlase, antiquary and writer on the history of Cornwall, who was rector of Ludgvan for 30 years. He had plenty of inspiration on his doorstep, with the Pendeen Vau Fogou; one of the most remarkable in Cornwall. It has a sloping passage 23 feet long, with a bend and a further 33 feet. The main passage is stone faced and roofed with lintels, and there is a 24 foot long chamber. A 'great wall' of turf-covered stones partly covers the fogou. These structures, still shrouded in mystery are thought to date from the Late Iron Age.

To the north west of Pendeen is a prominent headland with a lighthouse and fog signal station, built in 1900, known as *Pendeen Watch.*

Pengelly, *see* **Delabole**

Botallack Mine, near Pendeen

Pentewan

The now quiet, trim little village of Pentewan, meaning 'headland' or 'sandhills' pleasingly centred around its square and adjacent to the harbour, has its roots in antiquity. Prehistoric creatures once prowled the wooded lands now submerged by the sea, leaving bones and antlers to be interpreted by archaeologists. The village grew up around the knoll of an Iron Age settlement. During the Bronze Age the natural harbour was visited by traders in quest of the tin and copper needed to produce bronze. It has long been celebrated for its building stone, used extensively throughout the county, and particularly for 15th century church restoration.

An ancient overland route led over Goss Moor and Hensbarrow Down, and Pentewan was described by John Leland in 1549 as 'a sandy bay witherto fischer bootes repair for a socour.' In 1826 Sir Christopher Hawkins built a harbour for the export of china clay (see Par & Charlestown), and a simply operated railroad ran from St Austell down the valley of the 'White River', to Pentewan Quay. This railway, constructed in 1829, ran to a 2 feet 6 inch gauge. The trip down the Vinnick was an exhilarating one, much relished by the unofficial passengers, as summed up in this delightful piece of 1830 journalism: 'Considerable traffic is daily conveyed over the road which is in itself of admirable construction; but what renders it extraordinary is this, that four wagons linked together with about fifteen tons of china clay on them, are put in motion at the depot at St Austell by two men gently impelling them, they then move forward, their speed gradually increasing, and when they arrive at the lime kiln lately erected, a distance of two or three hundred yards, they proceed with the celerity of a mail coach. Sometimes twenty persons are seen riding on them at once. They continue thus to proceed for upwards of two miles, the man who has charge of them having to put his horse to a gallop in order to keep up with them. Having arrived at level ground, the speed of the extraordinary vehicles gradually diminishes until at length they stop, when the conductor attaches his horse to the foremost carriage, and they are thus drawn to Pentewan wharf . . .'

Locomotives were introduced in 1874, when unofficial passengers were paying 3d a ride. A saloon carriage was built for the exclusive use of the Hawkins family. Silting up problems with the harbour, accentuated by the indescriminate emptying of waste mica into the stream, together with tough competition from clay exporting ports to the east, brought about a decline, and the line closed in 1918. Pentewan was notorious for silting up and blocking the harbour entrance after a storm leaving ships marooned for weeks. In February 1862 shipmasters at Pentewan voiced great indignation about 16 small ships being detained here for 5 weeks, trapped by a sandbank, which the Harbour Company had not troubled to clear properly.

Percuil (Porthcuel)

The tributaries of the Percuil River, fed by numerous springs on the Roseland Peninusula, quickly incise themselves into the landscape, and emerge into Falmouth harbour between St Mawes and St Anthony headland. Early settlers who arrived by water established themselves on hilltops and around the creeks, and lived by farming and fishing.

In its sheltered situation, with a firm, gently shelving shore, Percuil offered an ideal landing place and trading point for the farmers and cottagers,cut off in this isolated area. Sailing barges and schooners beached here for their cargoes to be discharged into horse-drawn carts. Cargoes included coal, timber, building materials, grain, farm produce and manure, in the form of guano, imported from South America and transferred from ships in Falmouth harbour. There was a manure store here, fish cellars, and a store for the roadstone, brought round from the Porthoustock quarries by sailing barge, and used for surfacing roads in the Roseland peninsula. There was a limekiln just downstream. Oyster farming was traditional with defined oyster breeding beds and storage tanks. Percuil River oysters had a reputation for being free of contamination. The river was navigable, and shipbuilding and ship repair developed to meet the needs of the passing maritime trade. In 1888 the steamer *Resolute* started a regular Wednesday ferry service, leaving here at 9.00 a.m., and calling at St Mawes, St Just, King Harry, Tolverne and Malpas. If tides did not allow them to reach Truro Quay, a horse-drawn wagonette met the steamer at Malpas, to transport passengers on to Truro for a return fare of 4d.

Today Percuil remains a pretty hamlet in a delightful river setting, albeit with yachts and modern pleasure craft rather than the beautiful working boats that once anchored off.

Perranarworthal, *see* **Perranwell**

Perranporth

The Atlantic breezes shift the sands and ruffle the marram grass, as mighty rollers pound these shores. Thus did sand dunes gradually encroach and cover the ancient oratories here and at Gwithian, for St Piran's Oratory lies in the dune area between Perranporth and Holywell. Legend has it that St Piran floated over from Ireland on a millstone around 500 A.D., and built a church near the spot where he landed. This had to be abandoned in the 11th century because of sand encroachment, and a new church was built further inland. But this, too, was always in danger of disappearing beneath the dunes. In the 19th century, the sands shifted to reveal the secrets of the old Celtic church, and ghoulish trophy hunters dug up skulls and bones.

Perranporth lies at the point where two lovely valleys open out to reveal a broad expanse of sand, extending nearly 3 miles at low tide, from Ligger Point to Droskyn Point, with its attractive rock formations. Here industry has aided nature to create new forms of beauty, for some of the intriguing shapes, now mellowed and eroded by the sea, were 16th and 17th century mine workings, where tin, copper and silver bearing lead ores were extracted.

There was considerable surprise in 1847 when a large female figurehead was washed up on the beach. Another exciting happening, borne in by the sea was the appearance in 1879 of the Padstow smack *Willie* with a cargo of coal. Folk watched eagerly from the cliffs, but she had to wait for several tides before being able to come in and beach smoothly. A shoal of pilchards in 1884, which had attracted the abortive attempts of the St Agnes seiners, was later spotted off Perranporth. So a group of miners shot a seine and missed. Whereupon the fishermen, who prided themselves on their accomplished seamanship, and reckoning that miners might do well to stick to mining, daringly shot a 'Union' seine in a boisterous sea at low water on a very neap tide, when it was customary to wait for high water. To their jubilation, they enclosed a fine shoal, amounting to an estimated 300 hogsheads of fish.

Miners may not be the best of fishermen, but they had other skills. On one occasion, after a man and his young son were swept into the sea whilst loading pilchards into their cart, a miner called John Rippon heroically plunged into the water and hauled the lad into his boat leaving the father to scramble ashore. Another young miner, Thomas Mitchell, who knew where rare Cornish choughs were breeding on the cliffs, and had heard of the interest of the Prince of Wales in natural history, contacted him through his MP in 1863, and consequently had a mating pair sent to Marlborough House by express train.

As Perranporth became increasingly popular with holidaymakers towards the end of the last century, it was thought desirable for visitors, particularly ladies, that rules be laid down about bathing times. So it was decided that gentlemen could use the western beach until 9.00 a.m., leaving it for the ladies from then until noon. The poet Tennyson revisited Perranporth in September 1860, during a visit to Truro, and was 'greatly charmed with its fine scenery of sandy beach, lofty cliffs and extensive sea view,' and 'spent most of his time wandering about the sands in a contemplative mood.' He also made attempts to find the old church hidden beneath the sand.

In the village of Rose, about a mile to the east is St Piran's Round, a well preserved amphitheatre used for the performing of miracle plays, with a deep pit conveniently representing hell. Nowadays the four day *Lowender Perran Festival* helps perpetuate the Celtic culture.

Perranuthnoe

Perranuthnoe is at the head of Mount's Bay on the south-facing edge of a mild and fertile belt of agricultural land hence its exceptionally early spring flowers and vegetables. The village, clustered around its small church, is pleasingly situated looking down on a shoreline of blueish grey slate, reddish brown seaweed and sands which extend for half a mile when the tide is out. It commands stunning views of St Michael's Mount and Mount's Bay.

It was popularly believed that Scilly was originally part of the mainland, and that the once prosperous land of Lyonnese, with 140 churches, was engulfed by the sea, leaving only scattered hilltops, known to us now as the Isles of Scilly. The legend further tells of the sole survivor, Trevilion, who was miraculously borne to the safety of these shores by his trusty steed, in heroic style. Interestingly, the Trevelyan family arms depict a horse emerging from the pounding seas, supposedly bringing their ancestor to the Cornish mainland.

Nearby Acton Castle is a castellated mid 18th century mansion. South is the hauntingly beautiful Prussia Cove, formerly Porthlea, which derived its name from the notorious 18th century smuggler John Carter, who gained the boyhood nickname 'King of Prussia', inspired by Frederick the Great. He and his brother Henry became folk heroes with their colourful, swashbuckling exploits, bringing smuggling down to a fine art, with Henry proficient on the nautical side and John in charge of land operations. Although their armed vessels challenged revenue craft, and they served prison sentences in Brittany, they were never charged by the authorities here. When a consignment of liquor was appropriated by the Penzance customs officers, John felt his reputation was at stake. So he made a daring raid on the custom house to retrieve the goods.

Not all supported the smugglers. In 1857 the rector spotted a 112 gallon cask of spirits bobbing on the sea. With help, he landed and loaded it on a cart ready to hand over to Customs. However, word had got about, and there was a great commotion as men, women and children armed with pails and pitchers, staves and hatchets arrived on the shore, keen to exploit a promising situation. As the vicar struggled with the horse and cart, some artful person dislodged the cask, which sprang a leak as it hit the ground. By the time the mob had departed there was little more than a punctured cask to hand over to the authorities.

Captain Thomas Gundry, a well known copper miner, who wished to retain close links with his profession in the after life, arranged for his remains to be deposited in a copper lode which, he said, ran though the churchyard of the parish. And when the time came, the sexton was proud to have located the exact spot.

Mount Malpas Ledge was the scene of a dramatic shipwreck in April 1947, when the old battleship *Warspite*, being towed to the scrapyard, broke from her tugs during a strong south westerly gale and became stranded on these rocks. The Penlee lifeboat *W & S* went to her aid, and rescued the crew of 8 in classic, heroic style (see Mousehole).

Perranwell

Perranwell was described in Murray's Hand-Book of 1865 as 'a village romantically situated in a deep bottom or dell, at the head of Restronguet Creek, which is here joined by the Kennall, a small stream rising near Carnmenellis, and working 39 water wheels in its course of 5½ miles.' It went on to comment that the large iron foundry harmonised with its picturesque environment of densely clothed trees, creepers and moss covered rugged rocks. The Perran Wharf Foundry was the concern of the Fox family of Falmouth, who also had extensive industrial interests in South Wales, which included iron mines, copper rolling mills and collieries. Copper ore was taken by ship from here to Swansea to be smelted, and coal and pig iron were brought back. Machines for the mines were produced here. Communications were good, with the old Truro to Falmouth turnpike road running along the head of the creek. The arrival of the railway brought a halt. But trade had traditionally been waterborne, and the now silted up creek with its outlet through Carrick Roads was its lifeblood. The lovely old Norway Inn at Perranarworthal recalls the days when Scandinavian timber was brought up by barge from the big timber ships anchored in the Fal.

When the gunpowder mills were established at nearby Kennal Vale in 1811, trees were planted to dampen the atmosphere and deaden the force of possible explosions, (of which there were quite a few). For the same reason, the doors of the premises were covered with layers of dampened hemp matting. There were also important gunpowder mills at Herodsfoot, Nancekuke and Illogan. Despite these hazards, the place was obviously conducive to longevity, for in 1827 it was recorded that an 86 year old man enjoyed a shave by an 85 year old barber assisted by a mere 84 year old.

Perranzabuloe

Perranzabuloe, to the south east of Perranporth, or 'Perran in Sabulo', meaning St Piran in the sands', refers to the saint, who, according to tradition, was transported here on a millstone in the 5th century, and built an oratory (see Perranporth). When this became buried beneath the sands, it was replaced in the 15th century by another, further inland, which had similar problems. The stones were carefully removed to re-erect the church here in 1804, with further renovations in 1879.

A Good Friday fair was once held here. In 1845 young Richard James was hurrying along the lane clutching 'four men's dinners' (2 pasties and 2 currant cakes, 3 in his handkerchief and 1 inside his coat to keep them warm for his workmates). Then along came one Nathaniel Lanyon, who asked whose boy he was, and what he had in his hand. 'F..four men's dinners,' the lad stammered. Whereupon Nathaniel declared that he was hungry, pushed him aside, made off with the pies, and Richard's pleas that they'd kill him when he got home fell on deaf ears. The law caught up with him a month later.

Phillack

The area of sand dunes northwards across the canal from Hayle is of ecological and scientific significance and Phillack, to the south is one of the Nature Conservancy's Sites of Special Scientific Importance, (SSSI). Phillack's 15th century church amidst the sand dunes was rebuilt in 1856. In its churchyard is an inscribed stone (7th – 10th century), a coped stone and a wheel type cross. This was the scene of a bizarre incident in 1844, when a group of sick people who had engaged a scatterer of witch spells from Helston to cure them, were brought here for the enactment of the removal of ill-wishing. They watched in terror as the spell breaker paced over the graves, making strange noises and gesticulating. It was recorded that windows and doors opened and shut at his bidding, and the images of the ill-wishers confronted their victims. And then the spells were broken and dissolved. Cornish folk were also very superstitious about their holy wells. Somewhat eerily, a man called Erasamus Pascoe, who used the well here for washing his sheep, met a sequence of unlucky events, culminating in the death of his son, and (if the tombstone bearing the same name is relevant), his own death two months later.

In the early part of the last century, a small, compact species of sheep producing top quality wool and good meat thrived amongst the sandhills and annual wool fairs gave wool traders a chance to assess the quality for themselves.

Philleigh

An aura of tranquillity and well-being pervades the charming Roseland village of Philleigh, set on a ridge above the River Fal, with its little church of St Filius, 16th century inn, Georgian former rectory and scattered cottages and farms.

A medieval road leading to the busy market centres and ports of Mount's Bay and points westwards ran through Tregony and Philleigh, and traversed the river at King Harry, which must remain one of the loveliest ferry passages in the country. The shingly shores of the Fal to the north proved a convenient beaching point when trade was by water, and coal and vital supplies were landed here. There were a number of small quarries around the area, as well as lime kilns. In 1819, two men attending the lime kiln were overcome by gas as they attempted to press down the burning lime to make room to put more on. They both slumped into the burning mass and were quickly reduced to ashes. It had been a case of tempers smouldering back in the 18th century, when starving miners, angry about the inflated prices of grain, stormed Philleigh and the surrounding settlements, looting barns and cellars and dealing roughly with anyone who got in their way.

If folk thought that bad luck was coming their way, they suspected ill-wishing, and poor people parted with their money or stock for the services of conjurors such as James Thomas, (Jimmy the Witch) of Illogan, who found the Roseland peninsula a particularly profitable place to ply his trade. Old habits died hard in this isolated region and Sophie Dowrick, who died in 1928, dressed in traditional black Cornish garb and gathered herbs touched by the auspicious nightly dew. But poor old Betsy Benarth, a one time occupant of Tolverne Cottage, who was suspected of being a witch, was not so lucky, for she was burnt at the crossroads which bear her name, where it is whispered, her restless spirit still walks.

In early times, the manor house of the Le Sor family occupied an elevated situation overlooking King Harry and Tolverne; a site now occupied by a farm. The Le Sor family, who did not go along with the church, were subject to harrassment by their counterparts. The manor came into the possession of the Arundells, when a female heir married Sir John Arundell. Their son Thomas inherited Tolverne and the manor of St Mawes. But it was looted and burnt down by Henry Bodrugan during the Wars of the Roses (see Mevagissey). The Tolverne branch of the family did not prosper. The manors of Tolverne and St Mawes were sold to Thomas Walker, an Exeter merchant, and it changed hands many times before becoming the property of Lord Falmouth.

Smugglers Cottage, Tolverne

Place, *see* Percuil

Point

The narrow channel leading up Restronguet Creek to the port of Devoran was only navigable at the top of the tide, and Point, halfway down the creek to the east, offered a convenient trading quay for the shallow draught river barges which plied the Fal and Truro rivers. Pretty cottages were built up the hillsides to house the river folk. Sadly, these and other properties in the area, now fashionable and highly desirable, are way beyond the range of local folk, born here.

In the middle of the last century, John Stephens of Devoran started a small shipyard on the deep water shores of Penpol Creek, at a place still locally known as 'Yard'. Here the Ferris family created some of the finest sailing vessels ever built in the West Country.

Poldice, *see* Breage

Polgooth

To the left of the old turnpike road between St Austell and Truro is the ancient mine of a most extensive excavation with 50 shafts, and one lode worked to a distance of a mile. The lodes intersected each other in an unusual way. After the principal shareholder and director visited Polgooth mine in 1847, they were so delighted that they decided that every man, woman and child employed there should enjoy a bumper celebration. So St Austell was bedecked and garlanded, and triumphal arches were erected along the route taken by processions, led by St Stephen's brass band. Then 500 or so invited folk, who had brought along their own plates, knives, forks and cups enjoyed a good feast. Pearl barley was plentifully added to the leftover broth, and given to the poor.

Astonishingly, in 1854, an adolescent lad who was crossing the 56 fathom level of an inclined mine shaft slipped to the 84 fathom, miraculously escaping without a scratch. When found, he was chiefly concerned about losing the candles and cap his granny had given him. Miner John Lean of nearby London Apprentice was not so lucky. As he and a workmate grappled to light a candle in Woodclose mine in 1884, some sparks must have dropped on the stored dynamite cartridges awaiting the next shift. Both men took cover from the explosion at the back of the level, and remained there for three hours, aware of the danger of the fumes if they attempted to reach the shaft, but Lean died soon afterwards. The name London Apprentice is evocative of young men like this, who travelled afar to seek employment.

The famous *Trewhiddle Hoard* was discovered on that estate in 1774, during the course of tin streaming operations. It included a silver chalice, silver cord, silver ornaments and coins, probably hurriedly deposited by monks fleeing from the plundering Vikings. The chalice and silver cord can be seen in the British Museum. In 1823 the 'Pentewan Tankard', dating from the Iron Age, was found at *Levalsa*. This is now in Truro's County Museum.

Polkerris

The lovely little village of Polkerris, with its cottages, small stone pier and sandy beach, set in a crescent-shaped cove on the western shores of Gribbin Head, grew up as a fishing settlement. But fishing declined in these little coves around St Austell Bay as the developing china clay harbours offered better opportunities for employment (see Par, Charlestown & Pentewan). The *Rashleigh Inn* recalls Charles Rashleigh, the visionary who created most of these opportunities. The new harbours attracted more and more vessels. But this area could be hazardous in stormy conditions, when it could be difficult to negotiate the entrance of Fowey harbour, and when poor visibility sometimes caused confused mariners to run head on to the shore, having mistaken Gribbin Head for St Anthony's Point, and Callyvarder Rock for Black Rock at the entrance to Falmouth harbour. Trinity House erected a red and white striped landmark on Gribbin Head in 1832 as a safety measure.

Shipwreck was common on these shores, and the lifeboat here performed heroic service. Lieutenant Else, RN Commander of the local Coastguard detachment was awarded the RNLI's Gold Medal, and his crew received monetary awards for the rescue of the crew of the *Providence* in 1826, and in 1829 the rescue of 5 men of the *Diligence* earned Commissioned Officer Thomas Cresswell the Silver Medal. In 1866 it was placed on record that the lifeboat had saved many a shipwrecked crew, including 22 persons from the barque *Dogdens*, and the brig *Westmouth*, wrecked on Par Sands the previous winter. Remarkably, during the latter shipwreck, an Italian sailor was plucked from the surf, with a kitten clinging desperately to him. The kitten and the sailor went on their way together, with at least one of them having eight more lives left in hand! The old lifeboat house now serves as a giftshop and cafe.

At Christmastide it was customary for the poor cottagers of Polkerris to be regaled with a plentiful supply of 'good old English fare' by the Rashleighs of Menabilly. Menabilly Barton was made famous by Daphne du Maurier as the Manderley of her romantic novel *Rebecca*.

Polmassick, *see* St Ewe

Polperro

Polperro has long delighted visitors as being one of Cornwall's most romantic and picturesque showpiece fishing villages, with colour washed cottages clinging precariously to the steep hillsides, overlooking the busy little harbour, sheltering the boats essential to their livelihoods. Old Polperro, where some of the houses overhang the stream, was the hub of privateering and smuggling during the 19th century, and the first Preventive Station was placed here for good reason. Not surprisingly, the place has captured the popular imagination, and became the haunt of writers and artists. Sir Arthur Quiller Couch, known as 'Q', and recognised as the first of the Cornish writers, was the grandson of Jonathan Couch of Polperro, student of medicine, and author of books on natural history and the history of the village.

To celebrate the construction of Polperro's *Duke of Cornwall Pier* on New Year's Day, 1861, folk gathered as flags were hoisted and salutes fired. Then they adjourned for tea at the Wesleyan chapel, sang a few hymns and listened attentively to a lecture on local history by Mr Couch. However, most of their celebrations were of a rather more boisterous nature. The Feast of St Peter's was a hectic, 3 day event, starting on the eve of the festival with men and boys dancing around a bonfire on the beach. Local lads decked themselves out in garlands of flowers and decorated birds' eggs and village girls donned beribboned gowns. There were stalls, peep shows, jugglers, fiddlers, ballad singers, boat races, wrestling and refreshments, culminating in the choosing of the mock mayor, which ended in a ducking in the sea. Shrove Tuesday offered another opportunity for the lads to let off steam, rushing around, knocking on doors and chanting:

'Nicky, Nicky Nan,
Give me some pancake, and then I'll be gone.
But if you give me none,
I'll throw a great stone,
And down your door shall come!'

Polruan

The delightful village of Polruan, with its steep, huddled streets and colour washed cottages focused on the waterfront, is situated on the eastern side of the Fowey estuary, opposite the town of Fowey. Massive castles here and at Fowey dominated the entrance to the river, where a chain was suspended to deter uninvited visitors by sea. It was Polruan's function to back up Fowey's defensive role, itself one of the earliest, principal sea ports of the kingdom. Fowey contributed more vessels than any other port in Edward III's attacks on France in 1346-8.

In 1860 farmers lent horses and local folk set their shoulders to the wheel in order to haul two 24 pounder guns mounted on gun carriages up the hill to St Saviour's from the quay. These had been presented to Polruan's Volunteer Artillery by the government. Three years later, 4 guns at Polruan, and 2 at Fowey were defending the harbour entrance.

Picturesque Polruan retains much of its historical, maritime and essentially Cornish character, despite the social and economic changes. Boats and boatbuilding are still a way of life here, but in these Conservation conscious days, visiting schools of porpoises would be regarded protectively, rather than being blasted out of existence to protect the salmon fisheries as they were in the middle of the last century. Many of those living in the area now 'commute' across the water using the ferry or a variety of craft. The Bodinnick ferry, about a mile upstream, dates from the 14th century, or possibly earlier. Much of this beautiful area is now in the care of the National Trust.

Polyphant, *see* **Alternun**

Polzeath

This popular resort lies with its wide expanse of sands on the east coast of the Camel estuary. The late John Betjeman, who spent happy childhood holidays here, drew upon these experiences and impressions in some of his most evocative poems.

The concept of self catering holidays, albeit with one's servants doing the work, started early in these parts, for an advertisement of 1847 extolled the virtues of a 5 bedroomed house, with 3 parlours, kitchen etc., to be let to the Gentry by the week or month.

This section of coast was notorious for its shipwrecks. Just before Christmas 1864, the *Lady Eliot* came to grief, overwhelmed by the 'roaring surge', which built up as the fast, outgoing spring tide met the waves being driven in by a north westerly gale. Two years later the barque *Juliet* of Greenock met a similar fate, leaving casks of rum to be washed up on the shore. One William Ham of St Austell drunk so much a stomach pump failed to save him, whilst others staggered round the beach.

Five of the Padstow lifeboat crew lost their lives in going to the assistance of the schooner *Georgiana* of Boston, Lincolnshire, in February, 1867, when their oars broke and the lifeboat was catapulted end-over-end in front of horrified spectators, as they tried for a landing at Polzeath.

Half way through the week-long festivities of the St Minver Feast, it became traditional for folk from several parishes to join in the 'wash away St James' fun on the beach. In 1867, an estimated 2,000 revellers turned up, having travelled here by wagon, cart, horseback or on foot.

Ecologically interesting reedswamps near here contain *Cyperus longus* and *Sparganium erectus*, and much of the area is in the care of the National Trust. There is an Iron Age fort on Rumps Point, the tip of the promotory to the north.

Ponsanooth

Ponsanooth, straddles the parishes of Stithians, St Gluvias and Perranarworthal, and incorporates in its name the bridge over the Kennall river, 'one of the finest watercourses in the country,' which was harnessed for industrial uses, before flowing into Restronguet Creek near Devoran (see Perranwell and Devoran). In 1816 the extensive Ponsanooth woollen manufacturing concern, which had been thriving for at least 200 years previously, passed to Mrs Susanna Williams on the death of 2 leaseholders. She then put it up for auction at the *Red Lion*, Penryn. In 1843, when the 5 storey woollen factory was under the ownership of Mr Lovey, a fire, supposedly caused by the spontaneous combustion of oily wool from the carding machines, destroyed much valuable machinery. Fire engines rushed out from Penryn, preventing the blaze from spreading to adjoining buildings where wool and tanned sheepskins were being stored. There were a number of industrial accidents around the area. Elizabeth Rutter's carelessness brought tragic results at the Kennall Vale Powder Mills in 1826, when she walked into the mill after roasting potatoes at a nearby house, inadvertently carrying a spark on her clothes. Before horrified workers could do anything to prevent it, there was an explosion. Four people were injured, with Elizabeth and a Mr Weeks dying a few days later.

The fine old family residence of Roscrow, to the south east of Ponsanooth not only commanded outstanding views across Cornwall, it also embraced several hundred years of Cornish family history, for it had been the home of the Roscrows, Pendarves, the Bassets and the Fox family. It also became the home of William Yates, one-time owner of the woollen factory. Local folk were horrified to learn that it was to be pulled down at the end of the last century. For a time, it was used to house Napoleonic prisoners of war.

Porkellis

Porkellis lies between Stithians Reservoir and Wendron, between tributaries flowing south westwards past Helston, to Loe Pool. The high points of Carnmenellis and Calvadnack and their archaeological remains lie to the north, while ecologically interesting Porkellis Moor is to the south. In the last century, unemployed miners reclaiming marshland on Ralph Williams' Lezerea estate came across a large number of adders.

The village was the scene of a disaster in 1858, when an old, covered over mineshaft caved in, threatening miners as a sea of slime and water shot into the mine, causing the terrified men to run for their lives. Seven were killed as they swarmed up the sump shaft, and the following Sunday the area was invaded by an estimated 2,000 ghoulish sightseers.

Porkellis folk built up a reputation for delightful carol singing at the Wesleyan Chapel which drew people from miles around at Christmastide. Then, having sung their hearts out, and listened dutifully to the sermon, some adjourned to the *Star Inn*.

Port Gaverne, *see* **Port Isaac**

Porth *see* **St Columb Minor**

Porthallow

At one time nearly every sheltered cove in Cornwall had its own fishing industry, and Porthallow, colloquially known as 'Pralla', supported a thriving seining company, with a seine loft where the beach cafe now is, next to the evocatively named *Five Pilchards Inn*, and brine tanks. The villagers lived by fishing, farming and quarrying, but spilt-over deposits of rock and rubble which found their way into the sea from local coastal quarries, washed up and caused a build up of grey, gravelly beaches, to the detriment of the fishing industry. Modern quarries have remedied this problem, and fishermen today haul their brightly coloured boats up the more steeply shelving beach by winch. They watch the weather signs particularly closely, as fishermen here have always done because the cove is exposed to an easterly wind.

Local men, renowned for their courage and seamanship, have long carried out heroic rescues along this dangerous section of coast, which includes the notorious *Manacles Reef* (see Porthoustock & St Keverne). A much needed lifeboat station was established at neighbouring Porthoustock, with the *Mary Ann Story* arriving on station on 28th September, 1869, manned by fishermen of both villages. The sound of the maroons would set Pralla men running over the cliffs to take to their lifeboat, dressed in cork lifejackets. During the terrible blizzard of March 1891, the 4 masted ship *Bay of Panama*, homeward bound from Calcutta to Dundee, was driven ashore under Nare Head, to the north, with the loss of 18 lives, including the captain and his wife. In appalling conditions, Pralla men went to her aid, trying to get a rescue rope on board from the shore. It was a heartrending scene as victims who had sought refuge in the rigging froze to death. Joseph Hendy James of St Keverne trekked through the blizzard to notify the Falmouth authorities. He was acclaimed a hero, and received a public presentation of a gold purse for his actions.

It was a great help to poor farmers in this remote and rural area when a new passenger steamboat *St Keverne*, began its regular service from Falmouth, in 1876. It called here and at Coverack, Porthoustock, Helford and Durgan, offering a reliable means of getting produce to market.

Porthcurno

Porthcurno, where a flower-strewn valley gives way to a coastal scene of incredible beauty, with cliffs, sands and a vast expanse of sky and ocean, is the idyllic setting chosen by Miss Rowena Cade for her open air *Minack Theatre*. It was inaugurated in 1932, magically combining art and nature, all sculptured from a natural amphitheatre created by the contours of the cliffs.

Minack Theatre, Porthcurno

Above the shore to the east, stands the famous Logan Rock, which was fabled to have once been used as a court, for no criminal, it was said, could ever make it move. Moreover, Dr Borlase, the 18th century Cornish antiquary had been so incautious as to state that nothing could remove the rock from its steadfast situation. However, Lieutenant Goldsmith, a nephew of the poet, Oliver Goldsmith, proved Borlase wrong in 1824 when he and some colleagues toppled it to the shore. He was obliged to replace it at his own expense, by order of the Admiralty. Traditionally it was said that Porthcurno folk knew that misfortunes would follow when a phantom, black square rigger emerged from the ocean, out of the evening mists, and wafted inland, across the sands.

In April 1870 work was going on apace with the laying of the telegraph land line from Penzance to Porthcurno, while the steamer *Investigator* was setting the shore end cables to connect with the floating telegraph station *Brisk*, conveniently positioned off Land's End, to serve the many homeward bound vessels. The idea was that passengers would have the option of coming ashore by tender, thus shortening their journey by catching the train from Penzance. The Gibraltar, Malta and Indian cables were *in situ* by mid-June, getting off to a good start with government and mercantile business, drummed up by the Franco-Prussian war. Devotion to duty was such that during the Great Blizzard of March 1891, when all transport and communication services had frozen to a halt, a zealous employee of the *Eastern Telegraph Company* set himself the formidible task of walking through the deep snow to Penzance, and thence on to Plymouth, to deliver 700 communications; a feat which he managed to achieve, despite the fact that many roads, railtracks and houses had virtually disappeared beneath snowdrifts. Porthcurno remains the terminus of the ocean cables linking Britain with international networks, and there is a *Cable and Wireless* Training School here.

The granite hamlet of Treen or Treryn, to the east has an interesting church. *Treen Mill*, documented before 1500, was operational until 1910. In the days before customs men were effective around these parts, the brawny seafarers of nearby Penberth were wont to go out to foreign merchant vessels, on the pretext of helping or seeking assistance, but with the intention of plundering them.

Porthgwarra

This lovely little fishing settlement, on a wild coastline 3 miles south east of Land's End, was said at one time to have been populated by Bretons, and their descendants. A mile offshore is the notorious Runnel Rock, scene of many a shipwreck.

In December 1882, the fishermen of Porthgwarra went to the aid of a barque in distress. Before they reached it, the barque had struck Kite Cairn and was being swept back out to sea. In a rugged feat of great seamanship, they rescued the shipwrecked crew shortly before the vessel disappeared beneath the waves.

The village was once known colloquially as 'Sweethearts' Cove,' after the ill-fated love affair between a rich farmer's daughter and a sailor. Although her parents disapproved, they met in secret, and vowed eternal love before he set sail. Every day she stood on the wild Hella Point, gazing wistfully out to sea, and eventually went out of her mind pining for him to return. One night as she lay in her lonely bed, she fancied she could hear him calling. She arose, donned her cloak and made her way down to the shore. An old woman on the clifftop saw her at the water's edge, as a young man rose from the surf, took her hand, and vanished with her into the breakers. Later that day, news reached the village that his ship had gone down, with the loss of all hands.

Porth Joke, *see* Cubert

Porthleven

Porthleven's harbour, on the eastern shores of Mount's Bay, was formed by the long, granite quays constructed up a narrow creek. The haven gradually shelved seawards, and could only be entered at certain states of the tide. From 1811 it had been understood that in the case of a number of ships waiting to enter harbour, shallow draught vessels should proceed first, and dock as far up as possible. This seemed a good idea in theory, but in practice a number of vessels grounded, and floodgates, a breakwater and new jetty were built.

The place lived by fishing and boatbuilding, but life could be hard. When the fishermen of Porthleven had been unable to put to sea for 13 weeks in 1852/3, and could not afford to repair their storm damaged boats, a public appeal was launched on their behalf. Porthleven boatbuilders had an enviable reputation for their professional skills, and East Countrymen would order their fishing boats from here.

This section of coast has been the scene of countless, harrowing disasters. It was while witnessing the 1807 wreck of The *Anson* here and watching a fire works display that Henry Trengrouse conceived the idea of firing lifeline rockets out to ships in distress; an invention which has subsequently saved many lives. Experiments with projecting the line were carried out across the mouth of the harbour, in the presence of the Mayor of Helston and other worthies, who watched as a man was conveyed twice across the entrance by flexible chair on two rollers, and twice on the surface of the water, encased in a cork corset.

When a gale of November 1810 threw a 3 masted Spanish merchant ship onto Loe Bar as well as a brig, it was publicly stated that they would not have come to grief, had the Porthleven harbour been completed to offer protection to such vessels. Interestingly, quantities of wine, which found their way ashore, had to be kept by the finders for a year and a day, to allow the rightful owners to lay claim to it.

A storm of 1912, which shifted silt between here and Loe Bar, revealed Spanish coins, giving rise to the nickname 'the gold mine'. Behind Loe Bar is the freshwater Loe Pool, fed by the River Cober. This area is of great ecological and geological interest, with its profusion of botanical, freshwater, saline and shore life, supporting a wide range of insect, bird and other wildlife in a unique transitional habitat. The lagoon and the movement of shingle is of particular significance to coastal scientists, observing the effects of storms and other natural and man made impacts on the coastline, and their implications for the future. Loe Pool is a designated Site of Special Scientific Interest (SSSI).

Legend has it that the mischievous Tregeagle, who sold his soul to the devil, and clumsily dropped a sackful of sand at the mouth of Loe Bar, is doomed to try and scoop it all up for ever more. When he gets depressed, his lamentations eerily fill the air. Similarly romantic is the claim that this was the place King Arthur's sword Excalibur was thrown into the waters – a claim also made for Dozmary Pool.

Portholland

The quaint and remote little fishing village of Portholland lying at the head of Veryan Bay, was formerly populated by a close-knit, God-fearing community of fisherfolk whose staple diet was 'fish and taties.' During the season they washed, cleaned and salted supplies of fish, to see them through the hard months of winter. One can evoke domestic scenes of cottage life, with blackened pots bubbling on the range and of woodsmoke mingling with the pungent aroma of the fish oil lamp, gently swinging as storm winds howl across the bay. It was in just such conditions in December 1830 that hurricane force winds and mountainous seas ravaged the Cornish coasts for over 24 hours, wrecking many vessels and washing the bodies of shipwrecked sailors onto the shores. This was the occasion when Lieutenant William James RN of St Mawes plunged heroically into the sea to get a line aboard the brig *Bon Pere*, in distress off Portscatho; a feat for which he was awarded the Lifeboat Institution's Gold Medal. In the course of this hurricane the French schooner *La Mayenne*, the Russian brig *Saint Nicholas* and the Danish vessel *Catherine Margaretta* were stranded on the beach here and pounded to pieces. The crews of the French and Russian ships were bravely rescued by local fishermen who took to the sea in frail craft swept ashore from the *Saint Nicholas*. The *Catherine Margaretta's* crew also managed to reach the shore. Wreckers who appeared on the scene could only be deterred from their objective by the revenue cutter *Adder* letting fly with warning shots.

Porthoustock

The small fishing settlement of 'P'roustock', set at the head of a longish inlet to the north of Manacle Point, was once a natural, deep water anchorage, providing inshore breeding grounds for mullet, lobsters, crabs and other shellfish. But fishing declined after the quarries were developed around the turn of the century, with quays being built each side of the inlet. Stone, mostly used as roadstone, was crushed and graded into 5 categories and carried by tramways to the quays, and loaded on vessels to be taken to points along the Fal and Truro waterways, Plymouth and other south coast ports, as well as the Thames and northern Europe. Prior to the last war, beautiful 'outside' sailing barges, including *JNR*, *Silex*, *Dorothy* and *Sweet May*, were a familiar sight. Sadly *Sweet May* met her end here, becoming a victim of the easterly storms which can be so hazardous for Porthoustock and Porthallow. Rock and rubble which spilt into the sea from the quarries, washed up on the shore, causing the beach to become higher and wider above the original sand, altering the course of the stream, and making it appear that the sea has retreated by affecting the tideline. Today's fishing boats are hauled up the steeply shelving beach by winch, as at Porthallow. These derelict quays have now assumed the charm of a romantic ruin.

This area, so close to the notorious *Manacle Rocks*, extending offshore from here to Lowland Point, has been one of Cornwall's worst areas for shipping disasters, as the churchyard at St Keverne so poignantly demonstrates.

In 1869 it was decided that a lifeboat station should be established at the head of the beach, and in September the *Mary Ann Story* and her crew were drawn through Helston in ceremonial style, wearing cork life jackets and holding their oars erect. Her arrival in Porthoustock was watched by a large crowd, and there was something of a carnival atmosphere as she was christened, launched and put through her paces. Other lifeboats to be placed on station included *Charlotte*, *James Stevens No.* 17, *Queen Victoria* and *Kate Walker*. An upturned lifeboat which had been a relief boat for the *Charlotte*, served as a picturesque dwelling below Seaview Cottage for some years.

The build up of the beach made it increasingly difficult to get the lifeboats across and into the water. The crew got on board while the lifeboat was drawn on 'skids' – planks of greased wood – across the hard, grey beach and into the sea. Helpers who hauled on the ropes were rewarded with half a crown. But the situation became untenable, and the lifeboat was withdrawn at the time of the last war.

Porthmeor, *see* **Morvah**

Porthpean

The popular little resort of Porthpean lies on the westward side of St Austell Bay, looking across to Gribbin Head. This area has been much favoured by smugglers, who had to vary their tactics when a preventive boat was stationed here in the 1830s. It became customary to sink roped and weighted contraband goods which were retrieved later. This challenge to the customs officers was met by their patrolling likely spots, probing the waters with grapnels, and carrying off any hauls to their custom house stores at Fowey.

Tides and currents tended to bring a variety of things in from the sea. One of the more interesting, in 1858, was part of an 8 foot high white painted female figurehead, holding a richly gilt cornucopia (horn of plenty) in her hand. She was passed to the Director of Wrecks at Charlestown. A few years later the delapidated hulk of a vessel, wrecked about a century before, was born in by a storm. It was reported that there was 'a varied assortment of very fine old oak and other wood' on board.

Porthtowan

To the north of Redruth, the emerging resort of Porthtowan lies along a narrow combe leading to the shore, where broad sands and rolling Atlantic breakers are a delight to surfers. In July 1856 these rollers deposited a pitiful offering on the beach, in the form of a decomposing young elephant, with its legs bound together, and a rope around its neck.

The hillsides, littered with romantic, derelict mining structures tell a story of this once prosperous copper mining valley. When decline set in towards the end of the last century, there was quite an exodus to the mining camps of Grass Valley, California, where miners from Porthtowan outnumbered the rest. They took their traditional standards with them. Sunday was the day to close the mines, don one's best clothes and attend chapel, as they had always done back home in Porthtowan.

Port Isaac

This quaint fishing village with its narrow, winding streets, and houses clustered up the hillsides, is situated on the north coast between Padstow and Tintagel. Its name is thought to have derived from *porth izic*, indicating a corn port, and its pier was constructed in the reign of Henry VIII. Port Isaac, Port Quin and Port Gaverne, once exporting Delabole slate, were usurped by the coming of the railway. Port Isaac Road Station, on the London & South Western Railway, increased the prosperity of the area. Local folk were kept busy transporting fish in carts and waggons from the quay. Herrings were sent to Exeter, Birmingham, London and other centres of population. It was tradtional for thanksgiving services for the harvest of the sea to be held in the church, evocatively bedecked in fishing gear, flags and flowers.

Fisherman Jackson May, otherwise known as 'The Terror of Port Isaac', after being charged with smashing another fisherman's lobster pot and helping himself to fourteen lobsters, asked the police officer who arrested him if he fancied buying a lobster. The officer declined and issued a counter invitation to accompany him to the police station. Although May insisted that he had found the lobster in a pool on the beach, the case was clinched when the clawless lobster was matched exactly with a lobsterless claw found in the broken pot.

The romantic charm of this dramatic coastline, that inspired John Betjeman's:

> A mist that from the moor arose,
> In sea fog wraps Port Isaac Bay . . .'

has long attracted artists. However, these subtle charms and the characteristically relentless storms have brought tragedy to countless ships and sea-farers. A lifeboat station was established in 1869, on land donated by Lord Robartes. The lifeboat arrived in style, with the crew dressed in 'white frocks and red caps, holding aloft their oars.'

Portquin lies in a tiny cove to the west of Port Isaac, between Kellan Head and Doyden's Point, with offshore rocks named the Cow and Calf. This magnificent section of coast is in the care of the National Trust. The ancient cross on the Portquin – St Endellion road bears the inscription *Brocagni hic jacet,* thought to refer to Brechan, a Welsh prince, and father of St Edelienta, patron saint of the church of St Edellion. About half a mile to the east is the 16th century farmhouse, *Tresungers,* which has an embattled entrance tower.

Portloe

The delightful little fishing village of Portloe, where pilchard seineing was carried out in the last century, looks eastwards across Veryan Bay to the Dodman Point, which has claimed many a shipwrecked victim. There was a curing house here, and fish once formed the staple diet. Pilchards provided food and oil for the cottagers' lamps, or could be exchanged for goods or money. The main shoals would appear off Land's End around July, and men gathered on the clifftops all along the coast would cry 'Hevva! Hevva! . . .' and give directions through a cornet shaped speaker as seiners took to their craft. Three seiners would work together to enclose the pilchards in their nets, which would be anchored on the seabed before emptying or 'tucking' began. In 1839 it was recorded that some Portloe seiners shot round to Gerrans Bay, watched critically by the crew of another seine, who, 'suspecting that a bungling affair was likely to be made of it, shot their seine round them.' Skill and timing was all important, for the first group secured about five hogsheads of fish, while their rivals caught more than three times that amount.

Port Mellon, *see* **Mevagissey**

Port Navas, *see* **Constantine**

Port Quin, *see* **Port Isaac**

Portreath

Lord de Dunstanville, Francis Basset of Tehidy, who was interested in Cornish mining and industry, set out to transform this quiet little fishing village into a viable port in 1760, with docks and a railway. The first iron rail of the Poldice to Portreath Tramroad was laid in 1809, and a tramway with a 3 foot gauge was in operation between Portreath and Scorrier House by 1812. The *Hayle Railway Company* opened several lines for mineral traffic in 1837 and 1838, with a branchline to Portreath, leaving the mainline near Illogan Highway. An incline of 1 in 7 took it down to the harbour.

The railway, with a drawbridge linking Hayle Foundry with Pool, then Portreath, was opened in 1837, when a demonstration engine so impressed everyone guns were fired and colours displayed. The line from Portreath Junction to Redruth was officially opened in 1838. Portreath harbour was expanded in 1800, 1824 and 1846. Thus the pier, harbourside buildings and inclined railway turned Francis Basset's vision into a reality. Much copper ore was exported to Swansea for smelting, while coal and timber for the mines was brought in.

Some folk saw the docks as a good place to enjoy a swim, but this offended the sensibilities of genteel Victorian visitors who wanted to enjoy a stroll along the quays. Pressure was put on the authorities to forbid such improper goings on. There were plenty of interesting diversions, such as taking a paddle steamer trip down to Cape Cornwall on Bank Holidays, watching the celebrated 'American Jumper' dive into the sea from the highest cliff or spotting seals swimming close inshore.

Portscatho

This lovely little Roseland fishing village, just seaward of Gerrans, has delightful, whitewashed cottages, set pleasingly at various angles, a tiny harbour, boats, lobster pots, and a small beach. The light is intense, and the dreamy quality of the bay across to Nare Head, Gull Rock, Middle Stone and Outer Stone, quite beautiful. But this was the setting for many a gruesome shipwreck.

The coastguard station was manned by a chief coastguard assisted by 8 men until the First World War. In February 1914, the German 4 masted barque *Hera*, fully loaded and bound for Falmouth lost her bearings when her chronometer went awry in squally weather with poor visibility. She struck the Whelps, a submerged reef surrounding Gull Rock and started to sink within minutes. Some of the crew made for the ship's boats, but they capsized, and these survivors and others scrambled onto the jigger mast. Shouts and the blowing of a whistle attracted help. The Falmouth lifeboat *Bob Newbon*, towed by the tug *Perran* arrived on the scene, and searched in the darkness for the wreck. Having located it, they were able to save all who had endured thus far. The wreck was regarded as a danger to shipping and was blown up by Trinity House.

A year later, when conditions of war prevailed, the Falmouth lifeboat went to the aid of another 4 masted barque, the *Andromeda*, which had arrived off St Anthony during a gale, signalled for a pilot to enter Falmouth Harbour, hove to but began to drag her anchors and ended up on Killygerrans Head, about 3 miles to the south of Portscatho.

Alert Boy Scouts notified the authorities. The Falmouth lifeboat was called out, but had to return to port. Then the Portscatho Rocket Brigade, which was able to get a line aboard in the darkness, rescued 27 people.

It was off this coast that the author and 3 other people experienced a sighting of *Mawgawr*, Falmouth Bay's monster (see Mawnan Smith) at 20.00 on Wednesday 16th July, 1985. It had been a misty, humid day, but the sun broke through in the evening, lighting up the sea, which was exceptionally calm. There was excitement, and stunned disbelief when a large creature with a small head, long neck, large hump and long, muscular tail visible just below the water was spotted from the cliffs. For several minutes it glided swiftly and smoothly on the glassy water, its head held high. Then it suddenly submerged vertically, dropping like a stone, leaving no trace of where it had been upon the water. It did not re-appear.

Portwrinkle

In the early part of the last century the remote section of coast between Looe and Rame Head was heavily involved in the smuggling industry. The little hamlet of Portwrinkle, to the east of Downderry, with its tiny harbour, grey sand and dark rocks, was a hive of fishing activity centred on the fish cellars, stores, boats and seines.

In 1858, William Colmer of Polbathick and some friends who had been working in the mackerel seines, landed their boat at the Long Stone, between Portwrinkle and Downderry to go rabbiting up on the cliffs. But after spotting the landowner, and making a run for it, Colmer made the mistake of stuffing his gun into his coat pocket, which went off as he jumped the stile, killing him.

The areas eastwards around Trethill Cliffs, Tregantle Cliff and Sharrow Point are owned by the National Trust, whilst the Ministry of Defence's firing range has played its part in preserving a section of coast from development. Tregantle Fort was built by French prisoners during the Napoleonic wars.

Nearby Crafthole, where there is an ancient cross, was a borough at the time of Edward II.

Poundstock

Poundstock, to the west of the A29, betwen Bude and Boscastle, was recorded as Pondestock at the time of Domesday. Its name is of Saxon origin. The church, in its beautiful, rural setting is dedicated to St Neot, and has interesting wall paintings. Pleasingly adjacent is the 2 storeyed 14th century Guildhall, with a high pitched roof and attractive windows.

Penfound Manor, to the east, was given by William the Conqueror to his half brother, Robert, Count de Mortain. The last of the Penfounds died in the poorhouse in 1847. The story goes that the place has been haunted since Kate Penfound attempted to elope with John Trebarfoot of Trebarfoot Manor. As she climbed from the window into the arms of her waiting swain, her father intervened with his sword, and that during the fracas, all three were killed. Some say that her ghost returns annually on 26th April.

Praze-an-Beeble

This granity old mining village with a long street, between Camborne and Helston, is thought to derive its intriguing name from the commonland (praze) round about. To the south west lie the wooded lands of Clowance; to the east and north east, an ancient settlement and a burial chamber. The headwaters of the Red River rise nearby. Praze, a stopping place on the Helston Railway had its station gaily decorated for its 1887 opening when an address was presented. Praze Station served the villages of Praze-an-Beeble and Crowan. Sadly the line is now closed. To show the village's loyalty and respect for the Crown, St Swithian's Fair was postponed for several days in 1830, on the occasion of King George IV's funeral (see Crowan).

Probus

The church at Probus, dedicated to S.S. Probus and Grace, was at one time attached to a priory founded by King Athelstan around A.D. 930. The church is constructed of Cornish granite, with pleasing proportions, and the tower is reckoned to be an architectural masterpiece. At 125 feet, it is the highest in the county.

A sanitary report of 1881 drew attention to the absence of sewers here. Contaminated wells were situated near refuse heaps, manure heaps, pig sites, privies and beneath the level of the churchyard. But Probus folk knew how to enjoy themselves. There were 4 fairs, with a Feast Day on 17th September. Hurling matches were particularly popular. it was customary for the farmers of the parish to meet the landlord at the annual tythe feast, to settle up for the previous year. The lord of the manor would start the new year in bountiful style by organising an annual supper, with plenty of mead, for labourers and their families. The Probus Grammar School, no longer in existence, partly incorporated the old, 2 storey workhouse.

Golden, once a seat of the Tregians, has a priests' hole, where Cuthbert Mayne, a Roman Catholic priest was hidden by Francis Tregian early in Queen Elizabeth's reign. He paid the price for doing so with 20 years' imprisonment.

The priest was executed at Launceston.

Quethiock

The little village of Quethiock lies amidst hills at the focal point of secondary roads to the east of Liskeard. The 14th century church, dedicated to St Hugo, has an unusual, thin west tower, and some interesting brasses, including one of 1471 to Roger Kyngdon, his wife and 16 children, and another of 1631, commemorating Richard Chiverton, his wife and 11 children. Also of interest is a Hiberno-Saxon type cross, with a wheelhead and scrollwork on its shaft.

Rame

The little village of Rame is situated high on the peninsula which juts seaward to the west of Plymouth Sound. Its slate-built 13th century church of St Germanus has a west tower and tapering spire, which has long served as a navigational aid. There is a ruined chapel, dedicated to St Michael on the headland, a coastguard look-out point, a ruined castle and traces of other defensive work.

Rame Head commands magnificent coastal views and is the nearest landpoint to the Eddystone. On 20th July 1588 the English fleet made their first encounter with the Spanish Armada, offshore to the south

Probus church

west of this point.

The Head forms a short, eastern arm of Whitsand Bay, which has 4 miles of sandy beach beneath sloping cliffs, now dotted with shacks and bungalows. This section of coast claimed many victims in the days of sail. Looe's lifeboat *Ryder,* which came on station in 1902, was promptly put through her paces when she went to the assistance of the steamer *Daisy,* wrecked under Polhawn during a stong south westerly gale. The lifeboat, which had almost stood on end in the heavy seas, was recalled, as the crew had been saved by rocket apparatus.

To the east is Penlee Point, where a sonorous note of caution fills the foggy air. Cawsand Bay was the principal anchorage for vessels before the construction of the Plymouth Breakwater at the beginning of the last century. It was from Cawsand that Captain Maitland sailed in *Bellerophon* after Napoleon's escape from Elba, and to Plymouth Sound that the vessel returned, with him as a captive.

Rebullus, *see* Goldsithney

Retew

A mining settlement arose around Wheal Remfry, to the west of St Dennis, in the middle of the last century. Attractive, substantially built cottages, mostly 'two up and two downers', were provided for the workers. Surprisingly, some of these remained without sanitation or running water in the 1950s.

At one time a factory here employed 25 to 30 workers from Fraddon and Queens producing casks for packing of china clay. A handsome, multi-storey corn mill, which operated until about 100 years ago, functioned as a clay store, and later as a knitting factory, producing interlock underwear. The factory closed around 1918, was ravaged by fire and became a favoured habitat of pigeons.

In the old days the children of Retew walked 3 miles to the school at Indian Queens, then situated on Goss Moor. On Sundays they were obliged to retrace their steps in order to attend morning service, Sunday school, then the evening service. A chapel was later built in the village. After the last war bakers, butchers and grocers came out from Fraddon, St Dennis and St Columb. It was still very much an enclosed community, where everyone knew all that was worth knowing about everybody else. Folk still met and exchanged gossip around the village spring, as they converged with their buckets. Old 'Boss' Hooper reputedly said, 'When the spring dies, the village will die,' and the first omens of this metaphorical draught manifested themselves in the late 1960s. Rumours were rife that they were all to lose their homes in order that the clay beneath their feet might be exploited. Rumours gave way to reality, for villagers were obliged to leave their homes as the bulldozers moved in. It happened gradually, and some were to have the strange experience of bulldozers working around them; living in a ghost village, with moorland winds whistling through the empty shells of buildings which had once been the homes of relatives and friends, then being moved to houses on the outer perimeter, while it happened all over again.

Today the hopeful traveller who follows the signposts southeastwards from Fraddon will be disappointed, for the village has now been erased from the landscape, and a 'No Admittance' sign bars the way. 'It's a funny thing,' declared one former villager, 'all the years we lived in the village, there was never any signpost. Now there's a signpost but no village!'

Roche

Roche, lying on the northern edge of St Austell's china clay district is well known for its rocks, outliers of the Hensbarrow Beacon, particularly Roche Rock, on which a hermit decided to build his cell. This towering mound has various stories attached to it. Some say it was the refuge of a shunned leper of the Tregarnick family, whose only ally was a dutiful daughter, St Gundred, who brought him water from the now vanished well below the rock, and occupied a nearby cell.

The annual feast day, held in the second week in June was a chance to dress up and celebrate, with leafy branches and standards much in evidence. The highlight of the occasion was a circle dance known as the 'Snails' Creep', where they followed the band and became knotted in a tight coil, which had to be gracefully unravelled. Snails were generally regarded as lucky.

One local carpenter was Thomas Bassett. After having a leg amputated above the knee, Bassett designed a false one which served him well, then went on to establish himself as a designer and maker of artificial legs, with self-activating knee and ankle joints.

Roche Station is on the old Fowey to Newquay railway line, which opened for goods and mineral traffic in 1874, and passengers two years later. The name of the station, originally Holywell, was changed to Victoria before the line was opened to passenger traffic, then changed to Roche in November 1904.

The claymining villages of Stenalees and Bugle to the south east, fringe the old tin mining area of Carclaze, and are well known for their brass bands. Stenalees derives its name from *Sten*, meaning tin, and *lys*, denoting court, recalling the old Stannary court serving the area.

Rock

An early route into Cornwall running through Delabole and St Endellion traversed the Camel estuary from here to Padstow by ferry. This popular resort amidst the sand and tamarisks with its Georgian, Victorian and modern development, has a wharf and quay recalling the time it was a thriving little fishing village. When the Mariners' Inn was put up for sale in 1854, it had its own brewhouse and offered 'convenient stabling.' Today there is a pedestrian ferry across the estuary, and the once work-a-day place has become a popular sailing centre.

Enodoc golf course, stretching northwards, alongside the estuary, is regarded as one of the finest in the country. The hamlet of St Enodoc provided the setting for Sabine Baring Gould's novel *In The Roar Of The Sea*, about wreckers on the Cornish coast. Sir John Betjeman loved this romantic area, and he and his mother are buried in the churchyard of St Enodoc, once engulfed by the sands.

Rockhead, ***see*** **Delabole**

Rose, ***see*** **Perranporth**

Roseworthy, ***see*** **Gwinear**

Rosenannon, ***see*** **St Wenn**

Ruan Lanihorne

Ruan Lanihorne is one of the waterside settlements of the Celtic saints, conveniently tucked out of sight from seaborne intruders at the head of the Fal estuary. Communications and trade in this part of Cornwall were essentially by water until around the end of the last war. Like the rest of the Roseland, the area was dependent on agriculture and pigs once ranged the lonely lanes. Orchard fruit, potatoes and early vegetables all do well here for conditions are exceptionally mild.

Lands here and at Tregony came into the possession of the Normans after the Conquest, and castles were built at the river crossings to strengthen their newly won holdings. A number of fulling mills harnessed the waters of the Fal, including one at the now vanished medieval village of Sheepstors, and another at Tucking Mill Creek. Freshly woven cloth was taken to them to be cleaned and dressed.

Ruan Lanihorne assumed more importance as the silting up process brought about the decline of the port of Tregony. A small quay (now ruined) was constructed to accommodate the shallow draught Truro River barges. Silt was excavated from the riverbed and taken to the nearby kilns, to be manufactured into the distinctive Trelonk bricks. This material was also taken to Penryn to be processed into concrete blocks. Traditionally, workers on the Tregothnan estate carried out the seasonal 'barking' of the oak trees, to obtain resin for tanning leather.

Robert Long, a 17th century Cornish pirate, who used to unload his booty at Percuil, was captured by naval vessels after a skirmish in Veryan Bay and hanged at the corner known as 'Robin Long', between here and Betsy Benarth (see Philleigh).

A mile to the west is the little village of Lamorran, idyllically set amidst trees on the shores of the creek. Its has a 13th century church and some romantic, ivy covered ruins. The area has remained unspoilt, as part of the Tregothnan estate.

Ruan Major, *see* Ruan Minor

Ruan Minor

Ruan Minor, on the Lizard Peninsula to the north of Cadgwith, has a tiny church dedicated to St Ruan and a Norman font. Churches dedicated to St Ruan or Rumon are common in Cornwall. In this vicinity the name is also recalled in Ruan Major, the small settlement of St Ruan, Ruan Pool and also a holy well.

The driver of the mail cart coming out from Helston in October 1895 ran through a violent hailstorm then witnessed the dramatic sight of the little thatched Ebenezer chapel of the Bible Christians on Ruan Downs being struck by lightning, which ripped across the building from one side to another. It burnt rapidly to the ground, but fortunately local folk managed to rescue the organ.

To the north are Goonhilly Downs with earthworks, tumuli and hut circles now dominated by the cluster of grand and futuristic 'saucers' which make up the British Telecom Satellite Earth Station, open to the public 7 days a week throughout the summer. Interestingly, the perimeter, unsullied by human interference has become a spontaneous nature reserve of rare diversity.

St Agnes

The former little mining town of St Agnes lies beneath the shadow of St Agnes Beacon, where the high moors confront the sea.

Mining was a way of life around these parts from early times, and the area was noted for the superior quality of its tin. The village of St Agnes, situated high above the sea, and about a mile inland, has attractive miners' cottages clinging to its 'stippy stappy' streets. The beautiful Trevaunance Cove, adjacent, to the north, and now well known to holiday makers, has an interesting industrial past. Several attemps to construct a harbour here in the 17th and early 18th centuries were thwarted by storm damage. But when mining was enjoying a boom at the end of the 18th century, a small harbour was created. Copper and tin were exported, and commodities such as coal, timber and cloth were brought in.

The preacher John Wesley had a disquieting experience when he visited St Agnes, for being in need of accommodation for the night, he was obliged to take shelter in a reputedly haunted house. Awakening at midnight, he arose to find the hall full of gaily clad folk, including a gentleman sporting a red feather in his cap, about to lay into a tempting banquet set out on the table. On being invited to join in, Wesley insisted on saying the blessing before they began to eat. The guests stood, to join in him prayer, but when he opened his eyes, the room was in darkness, and the ghostly company faded away. Another ghost, said to be that of an old witch, reputedly popped up the mineshaft from time to time, to enter the Railway Hotel. Some believed her to be Dorcas, an old lady who once occupied a cottage at the foot of St Agnes Beacon, who, feeling depressed and lonely threw herself down a mineshaft. Thereafter she was said to call to miners, hindering them in their work, and giving rise to the expression that miners who slacked were 'chasing Dorcas.'

A colourful character around St Agnes in the latter part of the last century was Harriet Barkle, known to one and all as 'Lockett', who was in the habit of donning men's attire and doing men's work, such as driving horses, carting coals and heaving loads between the mines and the quaysides.

'Lockett' was obviously not the marrying kind, but the legendary giant Bolster was. In fact he made an annual habit of taking a new bride, having starved the previous one in the meantime. The story goes that he turned his undesirable attentions to St Agnes herself, but she artfully played on his vanity to dispose of him once and for all. Pointing out an apparently small cleft in the rock, she begged that he fill it with his blood to prove his love for her. What he did not notice when he adhered to her strange request was that the cleft was part of an open cave. They say that he bled to death and the sea ran red with his blood.

Harmony Cottage, between Mithian and Trevellas was the birthplace in 1761 of John Opie, who went on to become a fashionable artist. This son of a carpenter, known at the time of George III as 'The Cornish Wonder', was elected to the Royal Academy in 1787, and was buried in St Paul's. The airfield between Trevellas and the sea was a fighter station during the Second World War.

St Anthony in Roseland

St Anthony in Rosland was one of the original settlements of Celtic tribes who arrived here from Central Europe around 600 B.C., brushed aside the Bronze Age inhabitants and established themselves on their more favourable sites. It was ideal for navigation, with the advantage of being not directly obvious from the sea.

This delightful place, situated on a creek of the Percuil river was a monastic cell of Plympton Priory in early medieval times. St Anthony's 12th century church is plain, cruciform, aisleless, and has a broach spire. The adjacent Place Manor, now a hotel, was built for Admiral Spry in 1840.

St Anthony's headland commands breathtaking views of the coast, Carrick Roads and the waterways. It is said that smugglers watched the movements of St Mawes customs officers from here, relaying the intelligence by a system of signals. Appreciative crowds watched the placing of the enormously heavy fog bell on the top of St Anthony lighthouse in January 1882. It had been brought here by the steamship *Resolute,* and hoisted into position by a winch and a system of double pulleys. This area forms a key vantage point, romantic and historical. Henry Elger, 'The Old Man Of The Hill', who died at St Anthony in 1856 at the age of 91, could recount details of sea and shipping activity, and colourful characters, covering the previous century.

St Blazey

This village on the A390 has now virtually merged with St Austell. In the middle of the last century it may not have suffered from the volume of traffic it endures today, but the place was not lacking in hazards. The heavy horse-drawn china clay waggons played havoc with the road surfaces and caused innumerable accidents.

Exceptionally heavy rain in 1852 caused the bridge to give way, allowing a great surge of water to race through the village, with folk rushing upstairs to lean from their windows pleading for help. A boat took to the streets, rescuing trapped people, who were billeted in the National School for the night or cared for by friends. Several buildings collapsed, and some families lost all their furniture.

There were ugly scenes of industrial strife here in 1831, and the Riot Act had to be read, but without much effect. Arrests were made, and the mob made violent attempts to rescue the men as they were carted off to prison. Order was finally restored after 30 special constables were sworn in and the Royal Cornwall Militia placed on guard.

An off duty miner, James Collins, out gathering nuts, overstretched his reach and fell 70 fathoms down an old mineshaft. Having survived the fall, he determined to escape by climbing the shaft. He achieved this notable feat in just 10 hours.

St Blazey was the birthplace of Ralph Allen (1694-1764), who reformed the postal system.

St Breock

This pretty village at the foot of a steep valley lies on secondary roads just outside Wadebride. A stream runs through the churchyard creating one of the most attractive settings in Cornwall. It has associations with the Tregeagles, who somehow as Jan Tregeagle came to embody Cornwall's most infamous bogey man.

John Tregeagle, steward to the Earl of Radnor and wealthy magistrate used his power and influence to dispose of anyone he happened to dislike. He was responsible for the imprisonment of the simple girl Anne Jeffries, on the pretext that she was a witch. After returning to his court room in ghostly form and plaguing folk around the county the infamous Tregeagle is doomed to tackle impossible tasks to escape eternal damnation (see St Teath & Lanlivery).

Since early times man has left his imprint on this wild landscape, and St Breock Downs are rich in tumuli and stones of archaeological significance. An ancient route passed over Breock Downs, Goss Moor and Hensbarrow, down to the coast near Pentewan.

St Breward

St Breward, a long, grey, straggling, granity village on the windswept western edge of Bodmin Moor is also known as Simonsward. Archaeological evidence indicates that this was anciently the most populated part of the county. It was traversed by trading routes in the days of the old packhorses. Quarrying activity and prehistoric civilisations have left their marks on the landscape with tumuli, stone circles and hut circles. On King Arthur's Downs to the east is a rectangular enclosure known as King Arthur's Hall, while 4 miles north east near Brown Willy is Fernacre Stone Circle.

Across the moor to the north east at Advent lies the lovely little church of St Adwena, now without its village and standing isolated amid the fields.

St Buryan

The bleak, granite, upland village of St Buryan, about 4 miles inland from Land's End is particularly notable for its fine church, carved crosses and interesting archaeological sites. The church of St Buryan, one of Cornwall's best, is in close proximity to one of the most ancient Christian sites, where the pious King Athelstan built a collegiate church in about 930 A.D., in thanksgiving for his victory over the West Countrymen and their Danish allies.

St Buryan folk knew how to enjoy themselves. Horse, pony and donkey races were held in a local field and provided a fine opportunity for enthusiastic shouts, screams, the shaking of rattles and the blaring of horns. It was obviously a lively place to be. The irreverent old Cornish custom of choosing a mock mayor was relished.

The area hereabouts is particularly interesting for its history. The intriguingly named settlement of Crows-an-Wra means literally witches' crosses; Boleigh (or Bolleit), meaning 'the place of slaughter', is thought to have been the site of Athelstan's final victory in 936. The Pipers, supposedly the burial place of the victims, probably dates from earlier times. Also of interest are Trelew Standing Stone, a stone circle and *The Merry Maidens*. The whimsical story goes that a king's daughter together with her friends who danced on a Sunday, were petrified for ever for this sin, along with their pipers. Boscawen Un was deemed one of three places of poetic contest in Britain, where in 1928 the Gorsedd of the Bards of Kernow was revived.

In the church is the tomb of a Norman lady, Clarice, wife of Geoffrey of Bolleit, who offered ten days' pardon to whoever prayed for her soul. There is a roughly circular Cross Head outside the south porch, and a coped stone in the churchyard.

St Cleer

The upland village of St Cleer, which derived its name from St Clarius, lies in wild mining country at the foot of the moors, to the north of Liskeard. The church, with a fine granite tower, is reckoned to be one of Cornwall's best. In the last century, housemaids at the vicarage steadfastly refused to kill spiders, believing Parson Jupp's spirit to have settled inside one of them. This seems to be a variation on the superstitious theme of a spider spinning a web over the Christ child, to protect him from Herod. The holy well to the north of the churchyard is a pleasing 15th century granite structure, with a steeply pitched roof. The waters were reputedly capable of curing most ills, including madness. It was thought that illnesses would be discarded with handkerchiefs or personal items left strewn from the bushes.

After the exploitation of copper mining at Caradon Hill, and the construction of the *Liskeard & Caradon Railway* in 1846, the old tin workings around this area were revitalised. This brought about changes in the predominantly agricultural area, increasing the village population and establishing virtually new mining settlements such as Tremar, Hendra and Crows Nest.

The squalid conditions in some of these hovels brought early death to many of the miners. However, the *Mining Journal* recorded that: 'The change which the hand of science has effected here is a subject of great congratulation; the moors in the parish of St Cleer, barren and desolate in the extreme, on which nothing useful to the purposes of man was found, but huge masses of granite or scanty sheep pasture, which were as silent as they were desolate, have assumed a cheerfulness and activity, the result of noisy and busy labour.' It took over a century for ecologists and environmentalists to point out the vital part played by natural habitats such as this, and to change our attitudes towards 'conquering' nature.

Midsummer Day found the village festooned with wreaths of St John's Wort, traditionally acknowledged to deter witches. The evening bonfire was crowned with a witch's hat, while a sickle with an oaken handle was thrust into the flames.

Archaeologically interesting are Trethevy Quoit, a massive, closed megalithic chamber, described by Norden 300 years ago as 'a little howse raysed of mightie stones, standing on a little hill within a fielde,' three large stone circles known as The Hurlers, and the Doniert Stone, with an inscription telling us it was erected for the good of Doniert's soul, probably referring to Durngarth, the 9th century King of Cornwall.

St Clement

The delightful little village of St Clement is prettily situated on the tidal Tresillian River, to the south east of Truro, where woodlands descend to the shores, and the evocative call of wildfowl can be heard re-echoing across the water. Just up the hill, the churchtown clusters around the 13th century church, which was restored in Victorian times. The Polwhele aisle has a monument to one of Cornwall's notable historians, while the famous Ignioc Stone near the porch is regarded as the finest of Cornwall's inscribed stones. There is a lych gate built onto a cottage, with a slate-hung upper storey, which probably served as a schoolroom or vestry. Charming cherry trees add an extra touch of spring magic.

In bygone days the tiny village lived by fishing and agriculture, and boats were drawn up upon the shore. The story goes that St Clement was martyred by Trajan, and supposedly cast into the sea, with an anchor and chain about his neck. To celebrate the feast of St Clement, it was customary for single men to enjoy a hurling contest with the married men. This usually involved skirmishing through the streets of Truro and getting plastered in the muddy river, much to the appreciation of their enthusiastic supporters.

St Clement

St Clether

The charming village of St Clether, perched above the young River Inny, is known for its holy well, housed in what is claimed to be the largest well chapel in Cornwall. The Welsh St Clederus of the Brychan tribe came here during the 5th century, and created his cell by the river. The well chapel, 1/4 mile to the north west of the church in a delightful setting, was restored in the last century by the Rev Sabine Baring Gould, who wrote about Cornwall's history and folklore.

St Columb Minor

Although St Columb Minor finds itself attached to Newquay these days, it still enjoys an attractive situation among trees and hills. Its church, dedicated to St Columba has a fine tower; one of Cornwall's highest.

In the 1770s, a comprehensive canal scheme linking Porth, near Newquay, with St Columb and Mawgan Porth began to take shape. A section from Trenance Point to Whitewater, near St Columb Major became operational, with barges which had wheels allowing them to negotiate the inclined planes. They carried stone, coal, sand and manure. The section of canal linking Lusty Glaze with Rialton ran through here. But the venture was short lived, for it closed in 1781, and has now almost vanished into the landscape.

Rialton, known as Reilton at the time of Domesday, was a manor of the priory of St Petroc of Bodmin. It was the summer residence of the 16th century Prior Vivian, and had a small holy well.

St Day

St Day, to the south east of Redruth, lies in an area once busy with mining activity, for in the middle of the last century the Consolidated and United Mines was yielding more copper per annum than any other mines. The workings, covering an area of 2 miles, and reaching a depth of 1740 feet, had a number of pumping engines and water wheels, for operating machinery and stamping. Iron tramroads linked the mines with the ports of Devoran and Portreath, from where it was shipped to Swansea. It was operational until around 1865. Abandonment of the mines in 1878, and emigration to the New World, left the population depleted, with empty houses, closed shops and an air of dereliction. The granite church of 1828 was dedicated to the Holy Trinity, an unusual dedication for these parts.

Miner John Moyle had a remarkable escape when his leg became caught in a moving chain, which dragged him 70 fathoms through a flat shaft, upside down to the surface. After the traumatic experience, he changed into fresh clothes and walked home. Workers at the St Day Fuse Works were not so lucky in 1875, when an explosion killed a young woman and injured everyone on the premises.

St Dennis

Whilst mining was in decline at the end of the last century, the china clay areas around St Dennis to the north west of St Austell were enjoying a prosperity boom, with full employment, shops, a post office and 2 hotels doing thriving business, as well as enjoying the advantages of a resident doctor. As the population increased, the villages of Trelavour, White Pit and Hendra expanded to converge with each other, and create a small township.

Squire Joseph Thomas Treffry obtained an Act of Parliament in 1844 to make a tramroad from Newquay Harbour to the clayworks on Hendra Down. The railway, similar to that constructed from Par up into the mining areas, opened in 1849.

St Dennis was disturbed by a series of earthquakes in 1860, during which 'the chairs, table with a supper party around it, the plates and dishes on the dresser tumbled and the bells tinkled . . .' There were ructions of another kind when, at St Dennis Consuls clayworks, Moses Kent was set upon and rendered unconscious by his workmates for refusing to join the union. On regaining consciousness he was threatened with murder unless he changed his mind, so he paid his half crown membership fee to save his life.

There was much flag waving in 1857, when crowds turned out to witness the opening of the St Dennis to Newquay railway. The carriages were drawn by horses, which were disconnected at various points along the descent, and 2 trucks carried their first batch of china clay for export. The arrival at colourfully festooned Newquay was marked by the firing of a cannon. But transport could create hazards around the area. In 1861 John Key and John Kent, both of St Dennis, were each fined 10/- for being dangers on the highway. Mr Key had been riding without reins, while Mr Kent allowed his waggon to make its own way through St Austell unattended, while he was nearly a mile away.

The church occupies the site of a prehistoric fort. Some would claim that the hill on which it stands has associations with Arthurian legend, being where Gorlais, King of Cornwall took refuge after placing his wife, Igerne within the walls of Tintagel, fearing that Uther Pendragon was becoming too enamoured of her charms. Unfortunately his scheme went awry, for the impassioned lover took Damelioc, killed Gorlais, swept away the defences, to have what he most desired at Tintagel.

St Dominick

Meandering lanes lead to the village of St Dominick, 6 miles north of Saltash. This fertile south facing area has long been famous for its fruit, flowers and market gardening. Sadly, the orchards have been depleted, but caring local folk are keen to protect the individual flavour of this corner of the Tamar valley, captured so magically in the paintings by Mary Martin.

The river was the lifeblood of the area, with Halton Quay to the south, and the now renovated Cotehele Quay being focal points of trade. At Cotehele in the 1860s, there were 7 limekilns, a large granary, a public house, brewery, malt house, stables, labourers' cottages, as well as stores for manure, coal, iron ore, timber and salt, and 'an excellent dwelling house.' The deep water berths, able to accommodate the largest river vessels attracted a busy trade. River steamers called here most days.

Cotehele, dating from the time of Henry VII, was once the seat of the Edgcumbes. The property came to them in 1353 by marriage, but the present house, built of granite, is Tudor. In the second half of the 16th century, they built another house at Mount Edgcumbe, at the mouth of the Tamar, which became their principal residence. Cotehele House came into the possession of the National Trust in 1947. In the riverside wood, a small chapel commemorates Sir Richard Edgcumbe's narrow escape from Richard III, when the sight of his cap floating downstream misled his pursuers into thinking he had drowned.

An incident to shatter the innocent quietness of the lanes between here and Ashton in 1870 involved some self righteous parishioners indulging in the age old West Country custom of 'riding', whereby effigies of adulters were carried on poles through the streets, to the accompaniment of shouts calculated to humiliate the victims as much as possible. In this instance, the 3 large effigies represented 2 men and a woman. But the incident rebounded on those casting the first stone, and the lampooners were each fined half a crown, plus costs.

To the west of the village at Dupath is a well with healing properties, thought to have been constructed by the monks of St Germans in the 15th century. It is housed in a small, square granite building, capped with a gable roof, and crowned with a bellcote type turret above the entrance. Pilgrims were immersed in the water.

St Endellion

St Endellion, to the south of Port Isaac, has a well kept church, dedicated to St Endelienta. The story goes that this saint lived purely on milk, and that she died of a broken heart after her loyal cow was killed by a farmer. It was her request that she be transported to her grave by 6 young bullocks. A marshy place which miraculously became well drained as her body passed over it was reputedly the site for the church.

A cross shaft at the crossroads between here and Port Quin, bearing an inscription, probably dates from the 6th or 7th century.

St Enodoc, *see* **Rock**

St Erth

Centuries ago the River Hayle was navigable as far as St Erth, where the attractive old bridge was referred to by Leland in 1538 as being 200 years old. But time and changing demands have wrought many alterations. A Redruth smuggler had cause to be grateful for its shelter on the occasion he was returning home on business with a tired fully laden horse, and a customs' officer hot on his trail. When he got to the bridge, he smartly dismounted, pointed its nose in the right direction, then concealed himself under an arch. After hearing his pursuer pass overhead, he nonchalently emerged, reaching home to find his horse had already arrived and safely delivered its consignment of kegs.

James Bawden, who failed to pay a fine imposed on him for being drunk, was placed in the village stocks in May 1862. These stocks remained in service for about another 4 years. The village was once famous for its copper mills, which worked in collaboration with the

Hayle copper smelting works. Here in 1767 was born Davies Gilbert, that illustrious son of Cornwall, who distinguished himself in the mathematical, scientific, political and cultural fields. In 1797, the famous Cornish engineeer Richard Trevithick (Junior), married the daughter of another famous mining engineer, John Harvey of Hayle, at the parish church.

The church, dedicated to the Irish Saint Ercus, has a 14th century tower with interesting gargoyles, and is battlemented, with pinnacles. There are some interesting crosses in the churchyard, and the village has some charming houses.

St Erth Station, formerly known as St Ives Road Station, was renamed on the opening of the new broad gauge branch line in June 1877. This was the last section of broad gauge railway ever laid. In the 1890s, St Erth and neighbouring stations took pride in the number of truckloads of broccoli being handled.

St Eval

Cornwall occupies a strategic position in relation to the Western Approaches and the country's defence, and St Eval, to the north of Newquay, was the site of an R.A.F. base in the last war, with the now disused airfield becoming operational in 1939. Momentoes in the church and service style housing, of a type alien to Cornwall recall those days. Also emplanted in the landscape is a defensive system from much earlier times, in the form of a small fort with a single rampart, known as Trevisker Round, designed to protect a prehistoric settlement from warring tribes.

The church St Uvelus, lying on a high plateau, has a prominent tower, familiar as a landmark to generations of seafarers. It was so important a navigational aid that Bristol merchants contributed to its repair in 1727. The church, at times neglected, received more attention in 1892, after its bells had been defunct for over 40 years.

Just a mile to the west are the famous Bedruthan Steps, where slate and shale erosion has weathered the rocks, creating arches, stacks and rockpools. The stacks attracted the legend that the giant Bedruthan used them as stepping stones across the sands. Hereabouts, the vessel *Good Samaritan* ran aground, but if the old rhyme is to be credited, the local reaction made a mockery of the Biblical allegorical meaning.

'The *Good Samaritan* came ashore
To feed the hungry and clothe the poor,
Barrels of beef and bales of linen, . . .
No poor man shall want a shillin'.'

St Ewe

St Ewe is an attractive unspoilt little village lying in the agricultural area to the west of Mevagissey. Its impressive church of All Saints, approached through an avenue of palms has fine carvings and some interesting monuments. Hugh Atwell, who was rector here from 1559 to 1615, was also a herbalist, who enjoyed the reputation of being a magician because of his high success rate.

Heligan House, to the east, at the head of a wooded combe, was built in the late 17th and early 18th century stable block with a bell tower. At Polmassick, to the south west of St Ewe, there is an opportunity to visit the vineyard and sample the fruit of the Cornish vine.

St Gennys

The tiny village of St Gennys is situated on the spectacular north coast between Boscastle and Bude, just inland from Pencannow Point, overlooking the wide expanse of Bude Bay, and commanding a fine inland panorama. Its church is dedicated to the martyr St Genesius, who reputedly carried his head after being decapitated.

St Gennys High Cliff, at 731 feet above sea level, ranks as the highest in Cornwall. It also figured in Thomas Hardy's novel *A Pair Of Blue Eyes*. This section of coast has seen many a shipwreck. One of Bude Lifeboat Station's most outstanding rescues was carried out by the *Elizabeth Moore Garden (2)* in 1896, when she went to the aid of the Danish barquentine *Thyra* in distress offshore, during a relentless gale. She took off the crew, and as it was impossible to return to Bude the lifeboat landed at Boscastle, and was returned overland to Bude.

Sections of coast around Crackington Haven were donated to the National Trust in honour of aircrews who lost their lives during the *Battle of Britain*. Crackington Haven is situated at the mouth of a romantic picturesque valley, with a stream cutting its way through steep, flower and bracken strewn terrain and high cliffs. The strikingly beautiful geological stratas are of particular scientific interest. Back in 1836 there were elaborate plans to create a new port at Tremoutha Haven, but they proved abortive. An unconsecrated graveyard here bears witness to the days before the church was obliged to accept victims of shipwreck in churchyards (see Morwenstow, Gunwalloe).

St Germans

St Germans, on the lower reaches of the River Tiddy to the west of Torpoint, and adjoining Port Eliot, is rich in aesthetic, architectural and historical interest. The original church here, dedicated to the missionary St Germanus, Bishop of Auxerre, was one of Cornwall's cathedrals of Anglo-Saxon times. There was ecclesiastical reorganisation in 1050, when it was united to the newly founded see of Exeter. Early in the 12th century, St Germans became a priory of Augustinian canons. Much of the Norman fabric remains today, and is considered to be the finest example of Norman work found in Cornwall. Unfortunately, the old Norman chancel 'fell suddenly down on a Friday, being shortly after a publik service was ended.' But it was quickly repaired. There is much of interest to be discovered in the church. The six gabled almshouses, probably dating from the 17th century are also architecturally pleasing, as is the thirteen arched railway viaduct over the Tiddy.

The famous old walnut tree at the foot of Nut Tree Hill marked the site of many a colourful fair, held on 28th May, when children enjoyed the delights of the basket swing suspended from its branches. The following day, a likely candidate, preferably the most inebriated to be found, was dragged from the pub, elected as mock mayor, and carted around the streets to make a public address to people. Spirits ran high, to overflowing. Unsuspecting lads who entered the village without displaying an oak leaf in their hats were liberally doused in the spring. There was more fun in October, when the Agricultural Society held its annual ploughing match. And there was an opportunity to compete in an art known as Whink Spinning, which was the spinning of reeds into ropes, for use in thatching. It was customary for the Earl of St Germans to round off the day by entertaining the district's reputable yeomanry at the Eliot Arms.

As recently as 1853, a husband of St Germans sold his wife to a labourer living near Bodmin for £1, and wrote out a certificate to that effect. But the registrar at Bodmin refused to marry the new couple, and warned them that any attempt to proceed would render them liable for transportation.

St Germans enjoyed the advantages of being on the Saltash to Truro section of railway, which incorporated some fine viaducts. Six, between here and Saltash were originally constructed of timber, and some passengers were nervous of travelling over these high, fragile looking structures. Unfortunately, just 2 days after the opening of the Plymouth to Truro line in 1859, an engine and the first 2 carriages of a train from Plymouth, shot off the line on the approach to Grove Viaduct, near St Germans, and ended up in the creek with its wheels uppermost. The driver, fireman and guard were killed, but the passengers escaped with minor injuries. This, and neighbouring viaducts were abolished when the line was diverted in 1908 (see Menheniot).

The priory of St Germans came into the possession of the Devonshire family of Champernowne after the Dissolution, and the property was exchanged and came into the Eliot family's possession. Extensive alterations were carried out in the 19th century on the mansion and estate, known as Port Eliot.

Moyle Almshouses, St Germans

St Hilary

This attractive little mining village of granite cottages with slate roofs lies to the north east of Marazion. An apt inscription over the doorway of the inn proclaimed:

'Come all good Cornish boys, walk in,
Here's a brandy, rum and shrubs and gin.
You can't do less than drink success
To Copper, Fish and Tin!

There are shocking accounts of drunkenness and domestic violence in mining areas such as this in the early part of the last century. One concerns a bullying husband of St Hilary, who took great relish in brutally attacking his wife with a knife and knotted cord. A crowd assembled outside, attracted by the noise of the fracas, and distracted his attention long enough for his wife to escape to her brother's house down the road, bleeding profusely. Miraculously, she survived the attack, but her husband, assuming that he had murdered her thought it prudent to disappear. In 1837 there was a sad case of 3 orphan boys, habitual pilferers, who were found hiding in a disused mineshaft near Redruth. The youngest lad was sentenced to 14 years, but this was reduced to 7 after the intervention of the vicar.

Aggression in these parts, was not just confined to young and weak victims. After Father Leighton Sandys Wason was forcibly ejected from his vicarage at Cury in 1919, for being 'too Popish', and suspected of being the Devil himself by some, he took refuge at St Hilary with Bernard Walke, who held similar Catholic views. Bernard Walke was a dedicated man, running a home for crippled children, and encouraging his painter friends to present their pictures to the church. But in 1932 the church was vandalised by thugs hired by religious bigots, and many beautiful things were lost. This regrettable state of affairs projected the little village into the national headlines, and for a while it was sought out by the curious. Horrified villagers did their best to restore the *status quo*. St Hilary also became well known for its delightful dialect plays broadcast at Christmas and on All Souls Eve.

St Ive

St Ive, between Callington and Liskeard, has an interesting church, thought to have been founded by the Knights Templar, early in the 12th century. It is considered to be a good example of the Decorated style, and has a tower with 12 pinnacles instead of the usual 4.

A party of cockfighting enthusiasts from Liskeard and Callington thought they had neatly evaded the law by arranging a secret fight in a nearby wood in the last century. But Inspector Currah of Liskeard, who got wind of it, appeared with seven officers in the hope of catching them red handed. The noise eminating from the cocks and assembled mob led them to think that the session was in full swing, but when they made their dramatic pounce, it was only to find them waiting impatiently for more contestents to arrive.

St Juliot

The church of St Julitta is situated on the northern slopes of the fast flowing Valency River, which runs westwards through a steep valley to emerge at Boscastle. St Juliot is immortalised as the *Endelstow* of Hardy's *A Pair of Blue Eyes*. For Thomas Hardy came here as a young architect to restore the church in 1870, and met his first wife Emma Gifford who lived at the rectory with her sister and brother-in-law, the rector. Emma later wrote that Hardy was no stranger to her, as she had already seen him in a dream, and was 'immediatey arrested by his familiar appearance.' Their courting took place in this impressive landscape, and Thomas Hardy drew on these heady, romantic experiences in his writing. They married 4 years later, but it was not a happy union. After her death Hardy returned to retrace their steps and his poignant memories of those halcyon days gave rise to some of his greatest poetry. He erected a monument to her in the church.

St Just in Roseland

The pretty village of St Just, straddling the main road to St Mawes and the approach road to King Harry Ferry, is best known for its 13th century church of St Justus, idyllically situated on the shores of St

St Just in Roseland church

Just Creek, off Carrick Sound. The atmosphere surrounding the area gives credence to the age old legend about the boy Jesus, coming here with his tin trading uncle, Joseph of Arimathea.

One can look down through the lychgate, which is higher than the church tower, across the steeply sloping, leafy churchyard to the sparkling waters, and muddy creek.

The deep waters of St Just Pool were considered as a site for a Royal Dockyard in the 18th century. In the last century quarantine vessels were anchored here. The boatyard, which has long adapted to the changing needs of passing maritime trade now caters mostly for the yachting fraternity. A philosophical note in the workshop states: 'If God had meant us to build fibre-glass boats, he would've grown fibreglass trees.'

St Keverne

The delightful village of St Keverne lies in a large parish containing some of the wildest and most beautiful sections of Cornish coast, including the notorious *Manacles*, about a mile offshore, mostly submerged at high tide, and scene of many a shipwreck. The church, which was collegiate before the Norman Conquest, was granted to the Cistercians of Beaulieu. It is the largest church in the west of the county, and proudly dominates the village, within its handsome square. The church spire forms a navigational aid, aligned with Mên Eglos (church stones), rocks which form part of the Manacles. St Keverne's churchyard is the last resting place for a host of shipwrecked victims. Amongst them are those who lost their lives aboard the troopship *Despatch*, and also the *Primrose*, which both came to grief in 1809. In May 1855 the emigrant ship *John*, bound for Canada from Plymouth became another casualty of the *Manacles*, with the loss of 196 lives, of which 190 lie here. Austin Pengelly in old age recalled being interupted helping his mother scald cream in their farmhouse kitchen in 1898 by urgent cries of, 'Wreck! Wreck! Wreck on the Manacles . . !' The cargo ship *Mohegan*, bound from London to New York had foundered. The impact caused the sea to rush in and submerge the engine room, plunging the vessel into darkness. The passengers huddled together on deck, as 2 of the 8 lifeboats were landed, but the ship went down in 20 minutes, with the loss of 113 lives. The vicar of St Keverne church reported that many of the bodies were impossible to identify because some rescue workers had divested them of their personal effects and valuables. Thousands of Cornish folk came to witness the gruesome spectacle of the bodies laid out in the churchyard before interment. The following May, the American liner *Paris* went ashore and again thousands made their way here to watch despite the storm. On this occasion, all were saved.

Who St Keverne was is unclear. However a story relates that St Just (from the Land's End district) helped himself to St Keverne's chalice after enjoying that saint's hospitality. Realising where it must have gone, St Keverne set off in pursuit, gathering stones as possible ammunition. He caught sight of his guest hurrying along clutching the chalice, but his shouts only caused St Just to quicken his pace. So St Keverne let fly with his stones, which fell short of their target, and landed in a field thereafter known as Tremen Keverne (the Three Stones of St Keverne). The stones met the rather less poetic fate of being broken up and used for roadstone in the last century. Curiously an old proverb stated, 'No metal will run within the sound of St Keverne's bells.'

Outsiders were once regarded with suspicion and uninvited suitors could well have found themselves being unceremoniously carted off in wheelbarrows by over-protective fathers and brothers. One mother of St Keverne, found weeping, explained that the cause of her distress was her daughter's unreasonable determination to go ahead with marrying a foreigner – a man from Cury, 8 miles away!

St Kew

Prehistoric remains, Celtic stones and crosses and a coverging network of old lanes indicate the village's earlier importance. This unspoilt, picturesque place, situated in a valley by a tributary of the Camel, also had the advantage of being close to the old railway line between Wadebridge and Launceston. Its prosperity was reflected in the large 15th century church of St James, which contains some exquisite old stained glass windows, a well preserved example of an Elizabethan pulpit and a fine perpendicular font. Also of interest is a coloured plaster Royal Arms of 1661 and the ringers' rhyme board in the base of the tower. The Ogham Stone, with its morse-like inscription, may date from the 6th or 7th century. The attractive St Kew Inn, The Barton and an unusually large, Georgian vicarage adjoin the church.

St Keyne

The little village of St Keyne, lying above the Looe River, has a station on the branch line southwards to Looe. But it owed its original reputation to its famous holy well, situated about a mile to the south. The poet Robert Southey wrote a ballad inspired by the legend that the first partner of a newly married couple to taste these miraculous waters would win supremacy in the union. This quaint notion captured the Victorian imagination to the extent that they flocked here by rail, on a kind of pilgrimage. Norden, the Elizabethan topographer wrote of it as 'a spring rising under a Tree of a most strange condition, for, beyinge but one bodie, it beareth the braunches of four kinds, Oke, Ashe, Elm and Withye.'

A former rector, William Lamb, who married during the reign of Edward VI, found his status illegal when the Catholic Queen Mary came to the throne. He and his wife were dragged from their bed at midnight and placed in the stocks by self righteous Justices of the Peace.

A hundred years ago, the Liskeard to Looe line, originally a mineral railway, had 5 of the smallest stations in the county, described as 'little tool sheds of stations,' with Causeland, just to the south the smallest. It had a few feet of platform, and a shed, built of old railway sleepers, which could accommodate up to 6 passengers. There was no booking office as the guard nipped smartly out at each station, collecting fares.

St Leven

This romantically situated little village lies up the steep road from Porthcurno beyond the entrance to the Minack Theatre. It has a handful of pleasing cottages and a lovely little church, snugly set in its sloping churchyard amidst the boulder strewn terrain. Bungalows, not in harmony with the environment, have been allowed to take root on the clifftop here.

On the south side of the church, a cleft boulder near the porch was reputedly where St Levan rested after his angling expeditions. There was an old saying about the Day of Judgement being nigh when there is room for a packhorse to pass through the cleft of St Leven's Stone. The remains of Captain Henry Rothery and his crew of the Liverpool ship *Khyber* wrecked at nearby Porth Loe Cove to the north of Gwennap

Head in March 1905, are buried close to the church wall. Twenty three of the twenty six men aboard were lost and it is said that the sound of a ghostly bell can still be heard from the grave.

Hurling to County, which involved teams of young men chasing around the countryside, through thickets, swamps, rocks, cairns and other wild terrain, clutching a large silver coated ball, and being tackled in rugby style, was traditional around these parts for centuries. The objective was to get the ball into a chosen goal, which could be a churchtower or gentleman's house several miles away. St Leven lads sometimes combined with those of Sennen to take on bigger places such as St Just-in-Penwith, for the 'St Tusters' was generally regarded as a team to be reckoned with. It was firmly believed that the victorious team would bring good luck to their village and the whole thing was usually rounded off with a drink or two of strong ale, usually provided by the squire.

St Mabyn

A network of secondary roads converge on the village of St Mabyn, near the course of the River Allen and the old railway, to the east of Wadebridge. The parish is liberally sprinkled with small manor houses, including *Tregarden, Tredethy, Helligan* and *Colquite,* all dating from the 16th and 17th centuries. It is said that a hymn was sung in honour of the church of St Mabyn when it was completed around 1500. But that did not prevent the tower being struck by lightning. There is an ancient cross in the churchyard.

The local smith not only shod horses, mended ploughs and harrows, he was also a dab hand as a dentist. As often happened in folklore, there was an on-going feud between the blacksmith and the Devil, the latter always dreaming up elaborate rouses to ensnare innocent folk. On this occasion they resolved to sort out a dispute by seeing who could reap an acre of corn in the shortest time. But the blacksmith had taken a leaf out of the Devil's own book by hiding harrow teeth to blunt his whetstone. The enraged Devil grabbed his whetstone and flung it at his rival. It came to a halt as an upright stone, becoming a protection against evil. And this, so they say, is how the tiny hamlet of Longstone came to get its name. A local farmer finally removed the stone, for granite, unusual in this slatey area, was useful in the making of gateposts and bridges.

The area across the River Allen lays claims to Arthurian legend, with Kelly Rounds, or Castle Killibury being cited as one of King

Arthur's chief palaces. Interestingly, the Celtic 'Kelly', denoting woodland, has been Saxonised as Killibury.

St Mawes

St Mawes, situated on the Roseland side of Falmouth harbour, was described by the 17th century topographer Leland as 'a fischer town callid S. Maws,' having 'a chapelle of hym, and his chaire of stone a little without and his well . . .' This saint is said to have been distracted by a seal whilst preaching. Not liking the competition, he grabbed a rock and hurled it at the creature. It missed, but still remains where it landed – the distinctive Black Rock at the entrance of Falmouth Harbour.

The village grew up in the shelter of its low, squat castle, built at the time of Henry VIII as part of his programme of coastal defences. Together with its twin fortress, Pendennis, it sands sentinel at the entrance to Carrick Roads. Built during the cannon and gunpowder era, it has a central tower with 3 lower bastions. This created a complex of defensive circles, able to deflect cannon balls, yet offering the widest field of fire from within. At the time of the Civil War it was attacked by Fairfax. The Governor surrendered without a shot being fired, while Pendennis stood out for a 5 month siege.

Life around the harbour had its hazards, as demonstrated in 1861 when coastguards indulging in firing practice from the castle hit a boat, seriously injuring a man on board. In 1884, when the castle was being manned by 2 gunners of the Royal Artillery, there was criticism about the extravagance of a weekly garrison boat being brought across from Pendennis to bring the men their pay, manned by 6 men and a coxswain. It was pointed out that one man could bring it over on the steamer for a fraction of that cost.

St Mawes was a Rotten Borough returning 2 members to Parliament from the time of Queen Elizabeth until it was disenfranchised in 1832. Even the most powerful were heavily involved in smuggling. Sir Christopher Hawkins, formerly Lord of the Manor of St Mawes and an MP for Grampound left a legacy of £600 to the Exchequer as a post-mortal conscience payment. The preventive service regularly patrolled the cliffs between here and Portscatho, but some of the officers were afraid to fall foul of the smuggling fraternity, or were corrupt. For their part the smugglers kept a close watch on the St Mawes customs men from vantage points such as St Anthony headland, and relayed the intelligence along the coast, with a system of signals. In 1814 customs officers over-reacted when they challenged Thomas James of Flushing, innocently returning home by boat, and shooting him dead. On this occasion the officers were imprisoned for murder. But the hunch of the St Mawes men paid off in 1839, when they went aboard the coal carrying schooner *Marie Victoire* off Malpas, and discovered that she had a false bottom, crammed with spirits. The vessel was cut up on the shore.

By the mid 19th century St Mawes was populated mostly by pilots and fishermen, and there were coopers, netmakers, boatbuilders and other maritime industries close to the shore. It later became the favoured haunt of the well-to-do, and retains a touch of 'class' and a certain Continental air to this day.

St Mawes Regatta, when the place was gaily decorated with flags and evergreens, provided an opportunity to cast care aside and make merry. In addition to gig racing and a galaxy of other attractions on the water, there was lively music and dancing, and amusing games such as climbing the greasy pole for a leg o' mutton and diving for apples, with the whole thing being rounded off with a dazzling fireworks display. The sailing traditions continue, with the *St Mawes One Class* boats much in evidence, and the re-emergence of gig racing. St Mawes has also retained its regular ferry link with Falmouth.

St Mawgan

Inland from Mawgan Porth, with its great Atlantic rollers pounding the shore, and up the lovely Vale of Mawgan or Lanherne is the attractive village of St Mawgan, in a contrasting and agreeable setting. At the head of the valley lies the market town of St Columb Major. The praises of the fern-filled Vale of Lanherne were extolled by the Cornish poet Henry Sewell Stokes. Murray's Hand-Book of 1865 considers it possibly the most beautiful combe on the north coast of Cornwall, presenting 'a succession of lovely scenery.' It goes on to tell us that the groves of Carnanton, were formerly the seat of Noy, Charles I's 'able though miserly and crabbed attorney general', whose heart at the time of his death was 'shrivelled into the substance of a leathern penny purse.'

The church, which has a fine, pinnacled tower, contains monuments to the powerful and influential Arundell family, who resided at Lanherne, reckoned to be the best collection of brasses in Cornwall. It came into the family's possession by marriage in 1231. They were also the owners of Trerice. In 1794 Lord Arundell gave sanctuary to nuns fleeting from the French Revolution. In Elizabethan times, when some priests found it prudent to turn fugitive, it is said that one of them was concealed in a chamber for 18 months. The Tudor mansion became a Carmelite convent.

The open, salty, windswept, hedgeless, treeless area to the south, with runways, hangers and a variety of huts was one of a string of vital Cornish airfields during the last war, and together with Culdrose, it remains operational (see St Eval).

In 1773 there were attempts to create a canal system linking Trenance Point with St Columb and Porth, near Newquay. A five mile section was briefly opened to Whitewater (see St Columb Minor). Today the long stretches of sand at low tide attract family holidaymakers. A century ago, John Hobb, a local beershop keeper was fined £2 for not only fishing out of season for salmon in the river as it flows through the beach at St Columb Porth but spearing them with a 4 pronged manure fork, and stuffing them in his pocket. His pleas that he just happened to come across them lying there as he was gathering sea-weed were discredited.

St Merryn

The village of St Merryn, 2 miles to the west of Padstow, has an area of war graves in its churchyard, mostly relating to operational flying accidents during the last war. For a Royal Naval Air Station was commissioned as *HMS Vulture/Curlew* from 1940 to 1956. There is an annual Royal British Legion Remembrance Service, to which those who served in the Fleet Air Arm are particularly invited. Another annual event, traditional in these parts, but stemming from happier origins was the popular hurling match, held on the Festival of St Constantine. It is interesting in a county so celebrated for its pies that the parish is noted for having a shepherd's cottage held on a yearly tenure of a pie, containing such unlikely ingredients as limpets, figs, sweet herbs and raisons, payable on the Feast of St Constantine, in short, a shepherd's pie rental.

Much of this parish fringes the coast, with various watercourses making their way to the sea to the north and west, and today the area is favoured by holiday makers. To the north west of St Merryn is Trevose Head, capped by its 69 foot high, white painted lighthouse, build in 1847.

In September 1889 a large steamship, bound for the Canaries, put into Treyarnon Bay, and sent a launch ashore. It transpired that they were landing stowaways who had decided to give themselves up as they were hungry. They were deposited here, and left to make their own way to Falmouth.

At a Lower Harlyn Farm is a field where quantities of Padstow-caught pilchards, intended for the Italian market but rejected on account of their price, were dumped and left to rot. The near-starving villagers were forbidden to have them. The story goes that a witch called Mother Ivy sought revenge by laying a curse on the field, to the effect that the eldest son of anyone thereafter attempting to cultivate it would die; a prediction which has been horribly borne out. A happier tale of Polmark relates to an 120 year old bottle of beer, held by the Hawker family of brewers. On being tested in 1888, it was declared not only to have retained its quality and strength, but to have acquired that little extra 'something', reminiscent of champagne.

Cataclewse was a medieval quarry, from which an attractive bluish grey stone, popular for church decoration was extracted..

St Michael Caerhayes

The tiny village of St Michael Caerhayes stands just above Porthluney and Portholland on Veryan Bay. The place, better known as Caerhayes or 'C'raze' was once known as Lanvyghal, meaning 'the church of St Michael.' The church is Norman, and contains monuments to the Trevanion family, who occupied the original castle. Other artefacts include helmets and a sword, believed to have been used by Hugh Trevanion at Bosworth in 1485. The property had passed from the Arundells to the Trevanions by marriage. John Trevanion, an ardent royalist, met his death in the siege of Bristol during the Civil War. After the demise of the last male Trevanion in 1767, the estate passed to John Bettesworth through marriage, and he adopted the noble name. The poet Byron was a descendant of the Trevanions. His grandfather, who eloped with a cousin, joined the navy and became an admiral, was known to one and all as 'Foulweather Jack.'

In 1855, Michael Williams MP, a descendant of John Williams of Scorrier, whose family amassed wealth in the copper mines of Gwennap, purchased the estate, thereby becoming one of the county's largest landowners. The present battlemented castle, with a neo-Georgian ediface was built in 1808, and designed by John Nash. It enjoys an enviable situation amidst gardens ablaze with camelias, rhododendrons and azaleas.

St Michaels Mount

St Michael's Mount

The romantic eminence of St Michael's Mount, rising majestically above the waters of Mount's Bay, was anciently known as 'the Hoar Rock in the Wood,' and there is evidence of a submerged forest nearby. It had been a small port trading with France and other Mediterranean countries since the Bronze Age and has long been a place of pilgrimage. For after some fishermen had a vision of St Michael, it became a sanctuary and shrine. Edward the Confessor gave the Mount to the monks of St Michael in Normandy, who founded a priory here. It was later owned by a succession of notable families. At the time of the Civil War it was held by the royalist Francis Basset. It came into the possession of the St Aubyn family in 1660, and has remained theirs ever since.

Royalty was often entertained by the St Aubyns, whose stylish barge was handled by six special boatmen decked out in their 16th century livery of scarlet coats, petticoat trousers, frilly shirts and black caps, displaying the St Aubyn crest on caps and sleeves.

The Mount, which is about a mile in circumference, has a small village and harbour on the landward side, reached by a causeway from the mainland at low tide. Horses, oxen, men and carts became casualties of the tide on many occasions, and local boatmen frequently assisted with rescues, often watched by crowds on the Marazion shores. Although there was water all around, adequate supplies of drinking water were hard to come by, and in the latter part of the last century water piped from an old mine adit at Ludgvan to Marazion was brought across the causeway. Murray's Hand-Book of 1865 tells us: 'At the base of the Mount lies a fishing town of 80 houses, furnished with a harbour capable of admitting vessels of 500 tons.' There was a Wesleyan chapel, 3 schools, a shop, bakery, inn and customs house. There was also a dairy, with cattle brought across the causeway each day to be milked. The present pier and jetty replaced earlier structures, repeatedly damaged by storms. There was a coach house and stabling. Before the tramway lift was built, packhorses hauled supplies up to the castle. When Queen Victoria visited The Mount, she declined the offer of a ride in the lift preferring to take the steep pathway to the top.

The Mount which was given to the National Trust by Lord St Levan in 1954, has become one of Britain's most popular tourist attractions. Visitors can get there by boat or walk across the causeway at low tide. The original causeway was constructed at the instigation of the first Archpriest William Morton, assisted by the Bishop of Exeter, who raised funds by appealing to sinners to donate money, as an act of piety. Today's visitors can take the steep path up to the priory, through an avenue of tamarisks and sweet smelling alexanders, with magnificient views in every direction. Particularly interesting are the two rose windows in the 14th century chapel and the lantern cross which stands before it, the armoury, the drawing rooms, the fascinating old prints of the Mount, the plaster reliefs of hunting scenes and the paintings by Gainsborough and the Cornish artist Opie.

St Michael Penkevil

This delightful unspoilt little village lies on a peninsula formed by the Fal and Truro rivers, and bears witness to a bygone age. This was a collegiate foundation of the 14th century. The church, much restored by G. E. Street in the last century, has memorials to the Boscawen family of nearby Tregothnan, one of the finest seats in Cornwall. Admiral Boscawen, otherwise known as 'Old Dreadnought', was one of the most distinguished figures of our naval history. Tregothnan, built in the Tudor style in 1816-18, was designed by William Wilkins, who was also the architect of the famous Gothic screen fronting King's College, Cambridge.

The pretty estate cottages by the church are early Victorian. Not so long ago fine folk in stylish carriages frequented these quiet lanes, and came to worship at the church. Tregothnan formed the venue for countless local, county and royal events. Fashionable folk attended balls and enjoyed river excursions with the gentlemen attired in dandified sporty gear, and the ladies in tasteful long gowns, wearing becoming bonnets and carrying parasols at just the studied, appropriate angle. Excursions to Truro were made via the ferry to Malpas, where a waiting carriage would pick them up.

St Minver

The pleasant village of St Minver, 2 miles inland on the eastern side of the Camel estuary, is dominated by its church of Menefreda, with a tall spire creating a well known landmark. Its first vicar, Sir Matthew de Saucta Minefreda took up his duties in 1227. A parishioner, John Randall, who died in 1733 obviously had his anxieties about Eternity, for he left 10/- per annum in order that the vicars preached a funeral service on the Feast of St John for the following thousand years. St

Minver had a Quaker burial ground and a well of St Jesus famed for curing the whooping cough.

Centuries ago Leland placed on record that the parish of St Minver had been 'much annoyed with sea sand.' Sections of hard rock, resilliant to erosion, created conspicuous coastal rock formations, but the less scientific may like to subscribe to the theory that St Menefreda caught sight of the Devil as she combed her tresses on the rocks, and that she defied him by flinging her comb at him. Realising that he was beaten, he smartly disappeared down a hole in the cliffs, still much in evidence. The Rumps Promontary Fort has 3 ramparts and ditches, and a single entrance. Iron Age pottery has been found here.

The parish of St Minver has long been used to the effects of sand and sea. Occasionally the sea has yielded up some treasure. In 1819 this came in the form of a box of figs, which found its way onto St Minver Commons. News travelled fast, and the result was a most unladylike affray between the hefty 'bal' maidens who worked in the mines and village maidens, who kicked, scratched and tore each other's clothes off their backs in a bid for the figs. The bal maidens emerged victorious, gleefully making off with the prize. On another occasion, bones salvaged from the cargo of the wrecked *Immacolata*, and useful as a fertiliser, were auctioned here.

In 1820, ferry passengers intending to cross the Camel enjoyed the comfort and protection of a newly erected 'house and stable' on a rock on the exposed sands, from which they could signal for a boat.

St Neot

The small village of St Neot, set in farming country on the edge of Bodmin Moor, derived its wealth from wool, and woven cloth being treated at the fulling mill, and the mining of copper, silver and slate. Its prosperity is reflected in the church which contains much of interest, particularly the stained glass windows which depict some of the larger-than-life legends surrounding St Neot. This saint, only 4 feet in stature, was said to have been a brother of King Alfred. He enjoyed the contemplative life, and liked meditating immersed up to his neck in his favourite well. An angel decreed that he should partake of only one fish a day, which in turn miraculously appeared in the well. Ever resourceful, he was able to harness a team of stags when a dastardly thief stole his oxen. Neotstow was a Saxon collegiate at the time of the Conquest.

The place bristled with supersititions about animals. Extracted teeth had to be hurriedly burnt lest a dog should swallow them. For if Man's Best Friend had your teeth, it was only logical that his fangs might take root in the space left in your mouth. Kittens born in May were drowned, for it was thought that they might attract vipers and vermin indoors. But beetles were much luckier. Folk took care not to kill beetles, for doing so might bring rain. Someone must have inadvertantly steped on a few in 1826, when a cloudburst near Dozmary Pool caused a torrent of water to approach the village in an immense wave, sweeping a small bridge away, and bursting into Captain Sibley's house, causing his household to scamper upstairs in fear of their lives, as furniture and possessions were carried off. Workers sought refuge from the torrent surging into Lampen Mine and the slate quarries.

One local character was an 87 year old called Lee who in 1835 married 22 year old Maria Inch, within a week of burying his second wife!

St Newlyn East, *see* **Newlyn East**

St Ruan, *see* **Ruan Minor**

St Stephen-in-Brannel

The village of St Stephen-in-Brannel, 4 miles to the west of St Austell, grew up around its church and cobbled square, and expanded during the 19th century with the exploitation of china clay. But it had its roots in medieval times, and metals had long been extracted here. It was found to be rich in iron, cobalt, nickel and other minerals. Radium was mined at South Terras until 1925.

Interestingly, the secret of producing finest quality pottery, or porcelain, originated in China and reached Saxony in the 18th century, when a porcelain works was established in Meissen. It was William Cookworthy, a Quaker chemist and potter from Plymouth, who hit on the formula in 1745, using an American potter's ingredients. His searches led him to the discovery of china clay at Tregonning Hill, to the west of Helston, and to this area. In 1768 Cookworthy took out his patent for the manufacture of porcelain, which was later assigned to Richard Champion. Local china clay was much sought after by the famous Staffordshire potters, particularly Josiah Wedgwood. By 1807 there were 7 shallow, but busy china clay workings here, where china clay was being extracted by a form of streaming. With the ending of wars in America and Europe around 1815 there was renewed demand for quality porcelain, and speculators who turned their attentions to Hensbarrow Down made fortunes from the venture.

Many of those who worked in the old iron mines emigrated to Illinois, where wages were three times higher and there was scope for acquiring land. Some returned, having discovered that they could not bear to be severed from the place where they had 'roots', and an identity. Several generations on, descendants of others still come here in quest of just that. This was the birthplace of Joseph and Silas Hocking (1850-1935 & 1860-1937), sons of a mine owner, who both became Methodist ministers and prolific writers, mainly on religious and historical themes, with a partly Cornish background. But they left the area as young men.

St Teath

A network of secondary lanes converge spoke-like, on the pleasing, slate built village of St Teath, to the south east of Camelford. This was the birthplace of Anne Jefferies in 1626. Brought up by the family of Moses Pitt, a local worthy, she suffered a serious illness at the age of 19, and thereafter claimed to have communion with the 'airy people,' and was able to perform miraculous cures. She did not accept money, prepare remedies, or seek fame, and she was a devout woman. Nevertheless, she was charged with witchcraft by John Tregeagle, and cast into Bodmin gaol (see St Breock & Lanlivery). Despite being half starved and ill treated, she emerged from imprisonment radiant, having been secretly tended by the 'Little Folk'. She went to Padstow, continued her healing, and lived to a ripe old age.

Another St Teath character to land in Bodmin Gaol was James Sibley, a miller and ringleader of a mob who gathered at Camelford in 1837 to intimidate the Poor Law Commissioners. A few years later, drink was to be the downfall of William Teague. He and a labourer named Gribble were delighted to find that a keg floating on the sea contained strong white brandy. It has obviously been jettisoned by smugglers when the revenue cutter got too close for comfort. Word got around and villagers flocked to Gribble's cottage, where he had taken to his bed in a drunken stupor. It was so strong that people started collapsing. But it proved lethal for Teague, who went to a neighbouring cottage, sat on a chair and died.

St Tudy

The pretty village of St Tudy, lying in an upland farming area between the rivers Allen and Camel, is centred around its church and square. Some say that Tinten Manor was the boyhood home of William Bligh, destined to become Admiral Bligh of mutinous *Bounty* fame, but he was baptised in Plymouth. The Bligh family lived in Tinten for generations, several of them becoming mayors of Bodmin.

St Tudy had its tranquillity shattered the night shopkeeper Mr Wright was weighing out gunpowder for a customer by candlelight. He spilt some on the counter, and a stray spark from his candle ignited the powder and blew up his house. Not surprisingly, he was gravely injured. Another villager, Samuel Cowling, who stole a live duck from a farm here in 1841, was found guilty at Cornwall Epiphany Sessions, on account of indisputable evidence. The duck had a deformity well known to the farmer, and when it died, the zealous policeman had it put in a glass cage, to place on display in the courtroom for all to see.

St Wenn

The little village of St Wenn lies in an exposed, but enviably tucked away situation in an agricultural area to the north east of St Columb Major. Its church of St Wenna was struck by lightning in 1663, which may or may not give meaning to the punning quotation on the sundial, 'Ye Know Not When.'

The Chapman family of farmers, who flexed their muscles tilling the land were well known wrestling champions, while the Pryne family of Rosenannon built up a reputation for charming ringworms, afflicting man and beast.

St Breock Downs traversed by an early route (see Pentewan), and very rich in prehistory, was described as being 'particularly black and gloomy' as seen from a distance. Unfortunately large areas of moorland habitat have been 'tidied up', to be exploited for production in one way or another. What remains is precious.

St Winnow

The church of St Winnow enjoys an idyllic leafy setting on the eastern banks of the Fowey River, close to the water's edge. It is mainly 15th century, with some Norman fabric remaining, and its restored rood screen is one of the few to survive in the county. Close by is the vicarage, and slate farm buildings, pleasingly mellowed with lichen.

The northern part of the large scattered parish is liberally sprinkled with tumuli.

Sancreed

Although the sea is visible from much of the parish, Sancreed, on the Land's End peninsula does not actually meet the coast at any point. Drift Reservoir, to the east of the village, is one of several created in recent years to cope with Cornwall's increasing demand for water, particularly during dry summers, when the population is swelled by an influx of visitors. This also provides scope for fishing and birdwatching.

The engaging name of Sancreed signifies a holy faith, and John Wesley, who demonstrated just that throughout his life, enjoyed an excellent sermon here, but as a member of a congregation, for once. The 15th century church occupies a lovely setting amongst trees, while the 2 early crosses in the churchyard are notable for being well preserved and beautifully ornamented. Sancreed has a holy well of St Euny, reputedly where wounds were healed, and visited by sick folk at certain times. The character and beauty of this area was an inspiration to the Newlyn painters. Bill Foss (or Frost) of nearby Tregonebris, in addition to being a stonecutter, blacksmith and clock cleaner, was also a clever rhymster. His impromptu verse, sometimes traditional, often had a satirical sting in the tail, and tended to offend people. Nothing was sacred; not even epitaphs. For example:

'Beneath this stone lies a rotten body,
The mortal remains of Betty Toddy;

This early 19th century rhymster carved a milestone at Crows-an-Wra.

These lovely lanes were formerly busy and dusty with the activity of teams of packhorse mules, making their way to the port of Penzance, for this was once a tin mining centre. The area contains a wealth of antiquities, including *Bartine Castle*, *Carn Euny*, *Carn Brea* several standing stones, and *The Blind Fiddler*, an isolated menhir.

Sandplace

This hamlet to the north of Looe, with its thatched cottages on the hillside, still enjoys the advantages of being on the Looe railway; one of the few lines to escape the 'Beeching' mutilations of the 1960s. Sandplace earned its name on account of the sand being dredged from Talland and Lantivet bays being brought here, at the head of the navigable Looe River to improve the quality of soil in the surrounding area. The transference of this trade to Moorswater, which became the head of navigation when the Liskeard & Looe Union Canal opened in August 1827, resulted in Sandplace not only losing its sand, but also its lime trade, for lime kilns were then constructed along the way.

Scorrier

Scorrier lies in a mining area between Redruth and Chacewater, on the A30, close to the by pass and to the Plymouth to Penzance railway. Copper from the area was transported to the harbour at Portreath by a mineral railway, constructed in 1809, and operational until around 1865.

Scorrier House was well known as the seat of the Williams family who amassed a fortune in mining, and acquired Caerhayes Castle (see St Michael Caerhayes). They kept a fine collection of minerals including large chunks of Cornish gold and silver. John Williams also produced a considerable quantity of copper penny pieces dated 1811, with a design of a steam engine house and 'Cornish Penny' on one side, and a tin, copper and fish motif, and the words 'For the accommodation of the county', on the other. But when he discovered counterfeit coins were being made in Truro in 1813, he issued a public notice recalling all his coins.

Seaton

The Seaton River flows due southwards, through the wooded Hessenford Valley, to emerge through the coarse sand and pebble shoreline at Seaton, to the east of Looe. This, like neighbouring Downderry and Portwrinkle is a modern resort with caravan sites, bungalows and chalets, with some fine houses scattered on the cliffs, commanding lovely views of Whitsand Bay. This bay has been the setting for many a shipwreck.

The indications are that the place was of earlier importance. In the 16th and 17th centuries the names Sothan and Sythye appeared on the maps. One explanation of its decline tells of a petulant mermaid blocking up the harbour to get her own back because a Seaton man displeased her.

Sennen

Sennen, or Sennen Churchtown, just east of Land's End, and the most westerly village in the county is claimed as the site of the Battle of Vellan Drucher, when King Arthur and seven Cornish chieftains defeated the warring Danes. The story goes that the blood flowed so freely that it powered the mill wheel (from which the battle derived its name), and gushed into the sea. No Norseman escaped. A victorious, celebratory feast was supposedly held on the large rock known as Table Mên.

Folk around these parts gleaned their livelihood fishing, farming, and weaving, and when their work became wearisome, they would sing to help the 'triddles' along. They were accustomed to hard work, but in 1879 a Sennen octagenarian amazed everyone with his mowing of corn, pooking of turves, cutting of furze faggots and other country accomplishments, sometimes assisted by a lady 'bidding fair for 70.' Poverty was rife among the large families, where it was a custom borne of necessity to place older children into farm service. The girls would help the farmer's wives around the kitchen, tend the poultry and livestock while the lads would work on the land and walk behind the plough.

It was customary for farmers to burn the yuletide log from Christmas Day until Twelfth Night. There is a delightful story of about 150 years ago, when a group of Sennen farmers assembled for a fine dinner, which included 'four and twenty blackbirds baked in a pie,' and having eaten their fill, they emerged into the farmyard at midnight to witness the apocraphal sight of oxen kneeling in prayer in their stalls, facing the east. Traditionally, rushes thrown on the fire foretold of next year's happenings, by the way they withered and burnt. Local folk also looked for the portents by running ivy trailers through a ring, then leaving them in a basin of water overnight.

When 3 of the church bells were found to be cracked, a century

First and Last House and Longships Lighthouse, Lands End

ago, 5 new ones were made, incorporating the old metal, at a cost of £180. So to partly offset this debt, the villagers hit on the novel idea of holding a boating bazaar off Land's End, with a small fleet of boats displaying a wide array of goods, ranging from candies and refreshments, to dairy produce and lobsters, crabs and crayfish.

As the railway brought holidaymakers to Penzance, Land's End found itself increasingly on the excursion routes. Fashionable folk had to leave their carriages at Sennen and walk over a mile to Land's End before the First & Last House was built in 1830 for their convenience. Somehow things escalated to the point where its natural beauty and grandeur became destroyed by the numbers of people it attracted. Not only that, it suffered by becoming a symbolic extremity, exploited primarily for profit.

A *West Briton* report of 1899 makes interesting reading: 'Of all the places in the vicinity of the Land's End none can compare with Sennen Cove, for here is perfect peace, a panorama of unrivalled loveliness. There are no char-a-bancs, no Thursday afternoon trippers at so much per head, no pier, and, greatest blessing of all, no marine band of exiled Germans with asthmatical cornets or broken winded trombones. There is no excitement, except the occasional shooting of a fish seine and its ingathering, no noise but the sea's rhythmic roll. The livestock which infest most lodging houses near London have not yet reached the Land's End; and the Cornish landlady, if she is a wretched cook, is scrupulously clean.'

The village of Sennen Cove lies scattered along the southern end of Whitesand Bay, but the older part clusters around the quaint capstone house, later used as a fishermen's store. A rock called The *Irish Lady* marks the spot of a shipwreck, of which she was the sole survivor. It is said that she returns to the rock, holding a rose between her teeth. Two miles to the west is the *Longships Lighthouse*, while 7½ miles to the south is the *Wolf Rock Lighthouse* to warn of islets, rocks and stacks. Sixteen miles due west of Land's End are the deadly *Seven Stones Rocks*, which have claimed many ships, including the oil tanker *Torrey Canyon* in March 1976, causing widespread pollution. In July 1881, watchers on the coast would have seen the telegraph steamer *Faraday* laying and buoying the second Atlantic cable between here and Nova Scotia, completing 30 of the 2,500 nautical mile total distance.

The lost land of Lyonesse is said to lie between Land's End and the Isles of Scilly (see Perranuthnoe). Some folk fancy they can hear the submerged bells of the 140 churches pealing in conditions of exceptional calm. Indeed, fishermen in days of yore claim to have seen the submerged rooftops.

An ancient right, disregarded by Sennen fishermen in the early part of the last century, concerned Lord Falmouth's claims to the second best fish from each boat and the worst fish from each boat, and for the use of the rope and the capstan for hauling up the boats. The fishermen reckoned that as they did all the work, and had maintained all the equipment, they should not be handing over their fish because of an outdated custom. Lord Falmouth took up the case in 1826 and a jury found in his favour, with the exception of pilchards, for it was argued that pilchards were not being landed when those rights were established.

Sithney, *see* Goldsithney

Sladestandge, *see* Egloshayle

South Petherwin

South Petherwin lies in uplands between the Lawley Brook and the Inny, tributaries of the Tamar to the south west of Launceston. It is an agricultural area dotted with attractive slate and granite farmhouses.

Nearby Botatham was the scene of one of Cornwall's best known ghost stories, coloured up by Robert Hawker (see Morwenstow), and forming the basis of a modern poem by Charles Causley. It seems that after Parson John Ruddle of Launceston had preached a funeral service here in 1665, he was invited to the home of an elderly gentleman, Mr Bligh of Botathan, and introduced to young Nicholas Bligh, who was troubled by a ghost as he walked through the fields to school. It was thought to be the ghost of Dorothy Dingley. The parson and the boy had several sightings of her before the spirit was exorcised by the Bishop of Exeter.

Stenalees, *see* **Roche**

Stithians

A network of narrow lanes converges on the village of Stithians, with its granite cottages, inn and church, lying in a mainly agricultural area above the wooded once industrial Kennell Vale, to the north west of Penryn. It is in a region of moorland, dissected by streams, paths, tracks and lanes, on the edge of the Gwennap mining areas to the north, and granite quarrying areas of Rame and Longdown to the south. Stithians Reservoir, lying in the shadow of Carnmenellis to the west, covers almost 300 acres, and offers opportunities for bird watching, fishing, sailing and windsurfing.

Although it has been a busy, work-a-day place, villagers never enjoyed affluence. In 1871 parishioners and the church authorities came in for criticism for not providing proper ropes for use at funerals. Having borrowed the bell rope, and knotted it up for the purpose, the frustrated bell ringers had to scramble up the tower and improvise as best they could. Another example of frugality was their food at the feasten day, which gave rise to the mocking rhyme quoted in A.K. Hamilton Jenkins' *Cornwall And Its People*:

'Sti'ans bugs, leathern jugs,
Sour milk and whey,
Maggots boilin' in the crock,
Sti'ans feasten day!'

Today the village is probaby best known for its *Stithians Agricultural Show*, held in mid-July and an opportunity for farming families to meet annually and catch up on the news and gossip of the intervening year.

Stoke Climsland

The hilltop borderland village of Stoke Climsland lies amid fine scenery, just west of the Tamar and north of Callington and commands fine views of Kit Hill and the fringes of Bodmin Moor. It lies at the hub of converging lanes, and important early access over the Tamar at Horsebridge, dating from 1437. Around here, Luckett and Hampt, early industrialism has given way to ivy clad ruins. This was the cradle of the prestigious bell founders *Pennington* of Lezant and Stoke Climsland, who, between about 1702 and 1818 cast 489 bells for Devonshire churches.

Stoke Climsland has enjoyed royal patronage since the 13th century, when King John's second son Richard, who acquired wealth from his Cornish tin mines, bestowed on himself the titles of King of Germany and Earl of Cornwall. Prince Charles, Duke of Cornwall, carries on those traditions today, and likes to have first hand experience of life on the Duchy estates. The Duchy Home Farm produces prize winning stock.

At the other end of the social scale, it was recorded that in 1848 a tiny 'one up and one downer' cottage accommodated 15 sickly human beings in conditions of appalling squalor, out of which 2 sets of twins emerged in the space of 2 years, among the other babies born in the same room. At the end of the 18th century, humble cottagers worked long hours spinning wool distributed by the spinning masters. But when supplies ran short, there was real hardship, and special assistance was given by the parish.

Village folk have long demonstrated their ability to sort out social problems. The cruel practice of 'skimmington' or the 'mock hunt', was once common throughout the West Country, when any hint of past scandal could be aimed at newly weds. This took the form of crude impersonators of the unfortunate couple being transported through the streets, to the delight of a jeering crowd. In 1880 six people who staged a 'mock hunt' were let off with a nominal fine, after pleading that the centuries old tradition they were following was longer established than divorce. An unofficial custom here concerned the poaching of trout and salmon from the Tamar, a practice discouraged by the Abbot of Tavistock Abbey, who had a dam built at Gulworthy. There was rioting as local folk attempted to demolish the barrier.

Summercourt

This main road village at the junction of the A30 and the A3058 is always busy with traffic, except for the day of Summercourt Fair, when the A30 is usually blocked off, and traders fill the streets. It is the longest established fair in Cornwall, and possibly the country, dating back at least to 1201, when it was mentioned in a court case. It was the largest of the sheep fairs, and like those of Mitchell and St Lawrence, held in the autumn. This was the main venue for cattle and horse dealers, who came from all over the country, and spent several days in the village, as well as being a hiring fair, where farmers and workers sought each other out. There were sideshows, waxworks, travelling theatres and fairs, boxing, wrestling, penny peep shows, the chance to gape at giants, dwarfs, fat ladies and freaks. Refreshments included beef, bread and potatoes, but 'Boiled roast goose' was the speciality of the 'Old Fair.' Many reckoned that they had not had a really good day out unless they got drunk on 'feerday.'

A. L. Rowse, that literary son of Cornwall recalled a rhyme of his childhood, which summed up the spirit of the old fair, keenly anticipated and savoured in retrospect:

"Ere we'm off to Summercourt Fair;
Me mother said 'Ess',
Me Faather said 'No;'
An' dash me buttons if I dun't go.'

A Summercourt landlord, who reckoned the occasion would fill his coffers, regretted the decision to remain open for the sale of beer on Fair Day in 1845. After a prankster started 'popping' folk down on the floor others joined in and the whole situation backfired, when scores of men, mostly miners, came crashing in through doors and windows, breaking the furniture, turning the inn into a battlefield.

Billy Treglase, who frequented these fairs offered advice to Summercourt ladies in the form of a ballard:

'All the women of Summercourt Fair,
I'll give 'ee advice then you can beware!
If you man do drink too much beer or gin
You must scat 'un down with a rolling pin;
So, women, I hope you'll follow this plan
If you should be plagued with a drunken man.

Mitchell, on the A30 to the south west, formerly Meideshol, had a fair and market established by Walter de Ralegh in 1239. But it was one of Cornwall's rotten boroughs and declined after its disenfranchisement in 1832.

Talland

A tiny fishing settlement grew up at the head of Talland Bay, between

West Looe and Polperro, in an area where smuggling was rife. The grand and distinctive beauty of East Cornwall's Talland Bay, with its high cliffline, has been the cruel setting for countless shipwrecks.

The mother church of West Looe and part of Polperro was built here. Legend says that a church was started at a place known as Pulpit, but the stones laid each day mysteriously vanished, and a disembodied voice was heard to urgently declare:

'If you will my wish fulfil,
Build the church on Talland Hill.'

This would account for it being near the sea, away from the centre of the parish. It was largely rebuilt in the 15th century. Its church tower is separate from the body of the church, and is linked by an arcade. The churchyard is unusual, in that it is terraced. Inside the church is the particularly beautifully carved 16th century slate tomb of John Bevill, a Sheriff of Cornwall and Justice of the Peace. The nearby former manor house of Killigarth passed to John Bevill's father, Peter, by marriage into the Beare family. Sir John Bevill Grenville, a gallant Cavalier, killed at Lansdown in the Civil War, was a descendent.

It was rumoured that the ghost laying Parson Dodge, who was vicar here from 1713 to 1747, was involved in smuggling, and found it prudent to spread alarming tales of demons in the lanes used for transporting contraband goods to help keep the coast clear (see Lanreath).

Temple

The tiny village of Temple, with its handful of granite cottages, chapel and tiny church of St Catherine, is set amid marsh and moorland, rich in tumuli and hut circles, to the south of the A30, between Bodmin and Launceston. It derives its name from the Knights Templars, who once possessed lands here and acquired wealth by tin streaming. In the 12th century there was a church and a 'commandery' here, which passed to the Knights Hospitallers when the Order was suppressed in 1314. In 1340 a chaplain, a preceptor, a brother and two servants offered hospitality to travellers on Bodmin Moor, who were grateful for refuge from the elements and the robbers who frequented the ancient routes. During the 18th century, Temple was famed as a type of Gretna Green, where the clergy could legally marry couples who presented themselves, without banns or licence. It achieved some notoriety as a place where 'irregularities were carried out with impunity,' and in this way Temple found itself absorbed into colloquial language, for it was said of wayward women, 'send her to Temple Moors,' which could be interpreted as a route to salvation or a skidpad to help them on the downward gradient.

Temple could be regarded as one of Cornwall's few deserted, medieval villages. In the middle of the last century the place had an air of dereliction, and moorland cattle trampled among the gravestones and mouldering ruins of the ancient abbey church. But it was virtually rebuilt in 1883.

Tinnell, *see* Botus Fleming

Tintagel

This windswept village on the Atlantic coast, 4½ miles to the north west of Camelford and situated 330 feet above sea level, was known as Trevena, but visitors tended to refer to it by the name of the headland. On the rocky promontory jutting into the sea across a narrow ithsmus are the remains of a castle, claimed to be the birthplace of King Arthur. There was an ancient drawbridge here, but in 1820 and 1846 there were great cliff falls. Tintagel Castle was constructed on the site of a Celtic monastery, functioning from around 500 to 850 A.D. By the mid 12th century, when the first castle was built, the headland was in the possession of Reginald, Earl of Cornwall, Henry I's illegitimate son. It was rebuilt and enlarged in the next century and the curtain walls and the main part of the castle on the mainland were constructed. It was further extended in the 14th century, but was in ruins two centuries later.

A path leads down to the shore, where Merlin's Cave can be seen, recalling Tennyson's *Idylls of The King* when Arthur appears to Merlin. Further to this Arthurian theme, the Fellowship of the Round Table erected King Arthur's Hall in the village, between the two wars. Its windows depict Arthurian scenes. Although there is no archaeological support for the Arthurian connection, the legend of centuries and the grandeur of the scenery capture the romantic imagination.

The quaint Old Post Office, built in the 14th century as a manor house, is now in the care of the National Trust.

Tintagel (Trevena), and neighbouring Bossiney achieved political distinction by returning 2 members of Parliament to Westminster until the Reform Act of 1832. There were 25 electors, of whom only 9 (from the same family) exercised their franchise.

Tintagel's church, dedicated to St Merteriana, and situated on the exposed cliff edge, is one of the most interesting in Cornwall, retaining some of its Norman fabric. On the cliffs, a barrow and Iron Age fort tell a substantial tale of prehistory. People who follow the lovely cliff walks are rewarded by some of Cornwall's most beautiful and spectacular scenery.

Tolverne, *see* Philleigh

Towednack

The 13th century church of St Tewennochus stands in a small patch of tamed greenery, amid a moorland scene of open uplands, granite boulders, swamps and narrow lanes, to the south west of St Ives. The area beyond is rich in archaeology. A Bronze Age hoard was discovered in the parish of Amalveor.

Cornish churches such as this, virtually without villages, denote the site of a Celtic hermitage. It was anciently known as Towynnock. The story goes that this church has a squat, unadorned tower because the pinnacles built during the day were removed by the Devil at night. It was further said that there were no cuckolds in Towednack, because there were no horns on the church. In the last century it was recorded that the interior plaster encouraged the abundant growth of the rare alga *Oscillatoria cynanea*, 'clothing the walls with a beautiful light sky-blue colour.'

In days of yore, worshippers were met at the church door on their feast day in April, by a fiddler or 'crowder', who led the procession. This festival, attractively named the 'Cuckoo Feast', is said to have originated when a villager holding a party on an exceptionally cold April day, attempted to warm things up by casting some faggots on some brushwood, causing a surprised sheltering cuckoo to emerge. In the tradition of the *Wise Men of Gotham*, Towednack folk reputedly tried to build a hedge around the cuckoo, in an attempt to capture eternal spring (see Gorran). This tradition led to outsiders mockingly telling foolish folk to 'go to Towednack Quay', or to pose the satricial question, 'Who built the hedge around the cuckoo?' To which some local wags have been known to retort, 'If we'd built another one, we'd 'ave kept 'un in!'

Treator, ***see*** **Trevone**

Trebarwith, ***see*** **Delabole**

Treen, ***see*** **Porthcurno**

Tregonebris, ***see*** **Sancreed**

Tregony

Before the silting up of the River Fal, Tregony, to the east of Truro, was an important inland port, with access through the Falmouth haven to the sea. Indeed, Tregony folk are always quick to point out that:

> 'Tregony was a thriving town
> When Truro was a furzy down.'

It was also a borough, albeit a rotten borough, returning 2 members to Parliament during the reign of Henry I.

The Town Clock was the cause of much wrangling, which erupted in 1861 when it was discovered that someone had broken open the door of its turret and made off with the weights and pendulum. To thwart a possible follow up to the robbery, Mr Bawden, who was the winder up of the Town Clock, removed the rest of the works, encouraged by a group of vocal and enthusiastic villagers. Five years previously, a large bulk of corporation property had been sold to Mr John Dunstone, who always insisted that the clock was included in the purchase.

The Sexton, elected mock mayor at the Feast of St James in 1835, in traditionally irreverent style adopted the role rather better than anticipated, for having indulged himself with his favourite tipple and been carted through the streets to make ridiculous speeches, he slipped as he stepped grandly from his mock mayoral cart, slumped beneath it, and had a leg broken as he was run over by its wheels.

The attractive 17th century almshouses with a wooden upper gallery, which are so much a feature of the former town, were rebuilt in 1895. There are some interesting old houses in Fore Street. Their church, dedicated to St James, became ruined, and Tregony folk used the church of St Cuby, at the top of Fore Street. The population of Tregony, like nearby Veryan, suffered much as a result of the Great Plague, brought here, so folklore says, on a dropped, infected handkerchief.

Tresillian

Tresillian, to the north east of Truro, evolved at the convergence of early trading routes by land and water. The Tresillian River, which as a tributary of the Fal, has access to the sea through Famounth haven, was once navigable as far as the bridge. Before the silting up of the river, schooners and Truro River barges beached here regularly, to discharge cargoes including coal and roadstone. The river barges ceased trading around the time of the Second World War. Motorists on the busy A39, which runs alongside the river for about a mile here, get a tantalising glimpse of this once work-a-day scene. The mudflats attract a variety of wading birds, while the wooded banks, and dank, walled lanes give rise to a profusion of beautiful mosses and lichens. A lovely walk via Pencalenick to St Clement and Malpas, traditionally enjoyed by local folk, offers the opportunity to savour the atmosphere.

Tresillian Bridge, well known to thousands of motorists usually oblivious to the bridge itself, has been the site of a key event in the county's history. For it was here in 1646 that the Royalist general Sir Ralph Hopton surrendered to the Parliamentarian Sir Thomas Fairfax, thus bringing the Civil War to an end in Cornwall. Adjacent to it is the gatehouse to the Tregothnan estate (see St Michael Penkevil).

Further to the tradition of communications, the Plymouth to Penzance railway line was constructed close to the village, with 2 fine viaducts crossing tributaries of the Tresillian River, with Polperrow tunnel, another feat of engineering, to the north west. In 1847, about 200 people gathered to witness the unofficial cutting of the first sod, dexterously executed by Mr Findlater, the contractor. Ale and wine were kindly distributed to the men – as befitted their status, and a banner bearing the inscription 'Brunel & Broad Gauge For Ever', was flourished. The wag who wanted to know who Mr Broad Gauge was, received the reply, 'Mr Brunel's pet child!'

The estate of Pencalenick, on the river's western shores, was originally the property of Samuel Foote; it later passed to the Vivian family. The house suffered a fire just over a century ago, and was rebuilt in 1881. At the beginning of the last war it was requisitioned by the army, and housed Italian prisoners of war. It later became the headquarters for US troops stationed in the area, while plans were being formulated for the D Day landings, with landing craft being constructed at points along the Fal and Truro rivers.

Tretoil, *see* Lanivet

Trevalga, *see* Boscastle

Trevellas, *see* St Agnes

Trevone

Trevone, to the west of Padstow, grew up as a resort with a good bathing beach, facing north westwards, on the shores of Trevone Bay, where the Atlantic rollers can be a fine sight in stormy weather. Boarding houses, villas and hotels took root, and the place has been a delight to generations of holidaymakers. Iron Age graves discovered here bear witness to a contrasting civilisation, placing entirely different values on the environment.

The hamlet of Treator was the birthplace of Sir Goldsworthy Gurney, the inventor of road steam engines, lighthouse signals and other ingenious devices. He was buried at Launcells.

Twelveheads, *see* **Gwennap**

Tywardreath

Tywardreath, meaning 'settlement on the sands', stands on rising ground inland from Par Sands where the shoreline has retreated. When a Benedictine priory was founded here soon after the Norman Conquest it would have been above the beach. The priory became one of the most notable of the monastic foundations. However, having amassed wealth, it became dissipated, and the brethren were reprimanded by the Bishop for their lax behaviour. The place was dismantled, and nothing remains today.

The ploughing matches held here in the last century must have created a fine spectacle, as they skilfully vied with each other to cut a straight furrow. The contest began at the sound of a bugle. In 1875 the Tywardreath Cottage Garden Society proudly described at the time as being 'not only the oldest of the kind in Cornwall, but also in England', was celebrating its 45th birthday in style. To enliven the annual exhibition, the Par Artillery band came along and the village ringers showed what they could do. Local folk enjoyed sporting and athletic contests, and the whole thing was rounded off with a fireworks display. An interesting feat of another kind was the 1,173 yard long Pinnock Tunnel, to the south east between Fowey and Par, which was the longest to be constructed in Cornwall.

Varfell, *see* **Ludgvan**

Round House at Veryan

Veryan

The pretty village of Veryan, enchantingly set amidst trees in rolling farmland, about a mile inland from the bay which takes its name, is well known for its thatched and whitewashed round houses. It was said that they had no north side for the Devil to enter, and no corners for him to lurk in. Furthermore the conical roofs of the houses were surmounted by protective crosses. These houses were built during the 19th century, but capture the spirit of earlier times.

Veryan had 2 holy wells. Its church of St Symphonian, which appropriately has a musical, whimsical ring to its name, was built to an unusual plan, and has traces of Norman work. It was restored in the 19th century, and again more recently. Veryan was struck badly by the Great Plague (see Tregony), 'Pestilent wort' or 'Plague wort' sprouting from Veryan graves, was used as a remedy during the epidemic, so the story goes. Almshouses built in 1956 , known as the Homeyard Houses, include 2 round houses, re-echoing the old style. They were built to house the widows of 6 Cornish seamen.

It is not surprising that this area, with its sub-tropical flowers and picturesque buildings, is steeped in romantic associations. According to mythology, Gerennius, King of Cornwall was buried in Carne Beacon, in a golden boat with silver oars, and wearing a crown (see Gerrans). Sadly excavations in 1855 revealed no more than a stone chest containing ashes.

Warleggan

Waters arising on Bodmin Moor near Blacktor Downs and Carnburrow Tor flow southwards on each side of the lonely little village of Warleggan. The 2 arched bridge at Pantersbridge dates from the 15th century, while Tregoffe, just beyond was an old manor house. In the last century, tin was being streamed at Treveddoe.

The village lies at the edge of the moor in an area used for cattle farming and dissected by heavily wooded valleys. In this relatively untouched area, plant and animal life has had the opportunity to become particularly varied and interesting. Not surprisingly, this somewhat eerie area, away from the mainstream of life, has given rise to fantasies and weird happenings. The folk of Warleggan were rather wary of going out o' nights, for fear of being 'piskey led', by disconcerting, dancing lights. This was no flight of fancy, for in marsh and moorland areas, lights, colloquially known as 'Jack o' Lantern' or 'Joan the Wad', were caused by marsh gasses arising from the ground, and seeming to dart about.

Warleggan's church of St Bartholomew had a fine tower, until it was struck by lightning in 1818. One section fell on the church, destroying the roof and most of the pews, causing damage estimated at £600. Over a century later, from 1931 to 1953, they were unlucky enough to be saddled with an eccentric vicar, the Rev Frederick Densham, who kept the church locked for much of the time and created a bizarre world of his own at the rectory, behind a high wire fence, and guarded by Alsatians. His dislike of his parishioners was matched by their dislike of him. In the absence of any congregation turning up to his services, he put up cardboard figures and preached to them instead. An entry in his service book summed it all up thus: 'No fog, no wind, no rain, no congregation. This pathetic man died alone in his rectory, now known as The Rookery.

Washaway, *see* **Egloshayle**

Wayton, *see* **Botus Flemming**

Week St Mary

The village of Week St Mary, sometimes known at St Mary Week, incorporates the Saxon 'wic', denoting a settlement, in its very English name. Tumuli, earthworks and a hill fort bear witness to the importance of this area to the south of Stratton. This large, airy, upland village, dominated by a church tower, developed as a market centre at the junction of ridge roads. Near the church are the remains of a Norman castle.

The village is invariably linked with the romantic 15th century 'rags to riches' story of the shepherdess Thomasine Bonaventure, a labourer's daughter, whose charms attracted a wealthy London merchant who happened to pass by. He sought her parents' permission to take her to London, to be employed in his household, and after his wife died, he took her as his bride. After his death, she married another wealthy man, and having become a widow for the second time, she made another prudent match with Sir John Percival, who became Lord Mayor of London in1498. On being widowed for a third time, the now wealthy lady had a yearning for her Cornish roots, and a desire to use her money for good works. She endowed a chantry and established a number of charities and it is likely that her fitting surname was attributed to her after she had fulfilled its promise.

Northeastwards, across the wooded valley is the village of Whitstone, which has an ancient church with a beautiful Norman font. It was claimed in the 14th century, that miraculous cures were effected beside the grave of Richard Bovyle, a former parish priest.

Wendron

Tributaries rising on the shoulder of Carnmenellis, Nine Maiden Down and at Carnkie, make their way through Porkellis Moor, to be joined by others rising near Crowan Beacon, and Polcrebo Downs and Wendron, before skirting Helston as the River Cober, and flowing into Loe Pool, behind Loe Bar.

This had been a long established tin mining area, with hundreds of families relying on the old mines for their livelihood. The miners suffered a setback in the 1830s, when their all important tin streams were diverted for use in the newly established mine, Wheal Friendship.

At the Wendron Consols Festival, a procession led from the church to the mine house, heralded by the rousing strains of the Porkellis Brass Band. They sat down to enjoy tea and cakes at long tables, and the occasion was rounded off with a Floral Dance, illuminated by the flickering light of blazing tar barrels. At St Peter's tide, the lads of Wendron and other mining villages, including Four Lanes enjoyed firing miniature rock battens called 'plugs'. Other folk were less enthusiastic about the custom. This was the day for the Mock Mayor ceremony, and the Cuckles Court, (which may have been derived from 'Cuckold's). Those sentenced, usually visitors to the village, would have their faces blackened.

In 1878, landowning Lord Robartes, who felt he had a responsibility towards unemployed miners and others, created jobs by letting them bring uncultivated land into production.

Canon Gilbert Hunter Doble, the acknowledged hagiographer, was rector here from 1925 until his death in 1945. His serious study of Cornish and Celtic saints made a valuable historical contribution, for some who wrote about such things tended to be carried away by whimsy. But those who enjoy the whimsical might appreciate the tales of Parson Jago of Wendron, a celebrated layer of ghosts in West Cornwall. Among his other performances, he was obliged to lay the ghost of a restless suicide named Tucker, who persistently arose from his grave at a nearby crossroads to plague travellers.

Whitewater, *see* **St Columb Minor**

Whitstone, *see* **Week St Mary**

Zennor

Zennor church town stands between dramatic granite cliffs and treeless, boulder strewn terrain, descending from the tors westwards of St Ives. This grim and awe inspiring area, rich in pre-history, is steeped in atmosphere and folklore. The small fields, enclosed by huge granite boulders cleared from the moors to allow cultivation, probably originated in Celtic times.

In the Middle Ages this was a cattle breeding area, linked by a track across the moors to Marazion, formerly an important marketing centre. In the 19th century, the emphasis was on tin mining. Life was hard, and local folk found it difficult to pay their church tithes with cows and calves. Humble cottagers kept goats up on the hillsides which were fattened up and taken to be sold at the market at Christmastide.

Zennor

This custom gave rise to Zennor folk being nicknamed 'Zennor Goats'. They were also dubbed 'Zennor Charmers' on account of their reputedly magical gifts. Zennor men had a reputation as drunkards and rabble rousers, creating havoc, particularly at New Mill, on the way to and from Penzance of a Thursday night.

Zennor men were famed for their singing. It was reputedly the mellow voice of the squire's son that lured the Mermaid of Zennor into the church, entranced by his singing. She was to entice him away to her watery domain beneath the waves; never to be seen again. A bench end in the church depicts her with long, flowing hair, and a comb and a glass in her hand. Buried in this churchyard are the two John Daveys, father and son (1770-1884 and 1812-1891), cited as being the last to understand the Cornish language (see Paul & Mousehole).

In common with other areas of Cornwall, it was customary for funerals to be well attended. Neighbouring cynics said that Zennor folk attended as many funerals as possible in order to get a good feed afterwards. But they would argue that with their fine reputation for singing, they were welcome guests anywhere. A sad tale of 1840 concerns a Zennor man who attended a friend's funeral at nearby Tregerthen. He was killed when the weight of the sorrowing family upstairs caused the cottage ceiling to collapse on him and other mourners. A bridal custom here involved newly weds being waylaid and whipped to bed with cords and handy implements, to ensure a happy and fruitful union. A slight variation on this theme involved the throwing of weighted stockings at the couple in bed.

The Zennor Quoit is a cromlech containing two sepulchres, covered by a big stone; the largest in the county. A rock formation known as Witch's Rock marked the meeting place of Cornish covens, which assembled there on Midsummer Eve. Touching the rock nine times at midnight was considered a protective measure against misfortune. On Gurnard's Head, to the west, was Trereen Dinas, one of Cornwall's famous cliff castles, with traces of the fortifications visible on the isthmus. It is a superb vantage point.

The village enjoys a variety of literary associations. The writer W. H. Hudson stayed here in 1906 while researching material for his book *The Land's End, a Naturalists' Impressions In West Cornwall* (1908), and a plaque near the old quarry commemorates the place where he sat and observed the wildlife. D. H. Lawrence and his German wife Frieda stopped at the *Tinners' Arms* in 1916, while prospecting for a cottage to rent. Having moved into one of a pair of small cottages at Higher Tregerthen they invited Katherine Mansfield and John Middleton Murry to occupy the other, hoping to establish a small core of kindred spirits. However, the newcomers stayed only briefly, before moving on to Mylor. The anti-war intellectual and his wife were regarded with suspicion by the local folk, who thought that they were signalling to German submarines from their cottage window. In 1917 they felt obliged to go. Much of Lawrence's novel *Women in Love* was written during this period. Zennor was in 1792, the birthplace of Henna (Henry) Quick, who was one of Cornwall's outstanding rhymsters, displaying sharp wit and a good command of language. Although his work was fresh and original, deftly catching the essence of country life in Cornwall, with some shrewd observations, he remained closer to his mother than anyone else. Realising even then, the threats to Cornwall and its culture he wrote:

'The Cornish drolls are dead, each one;
The fairies from their haunts have gone:
There's scarce a witch in all the land,
The world has grown so learn'd and grand.'

Bibliography

Anthony, G. H., The Hayle, West Cornwall & Helston Railway, 1968
Balchin, W. G. V., The Cornish Landscape, 1983
Barton, D. B., The Redruth & Chacewater Railway, 1824-1915
Barton, R. M., Life In Cornwall: In The Early 19th Century, 1970
Barton, R. M., Life In Cornwall: In The Mid 19th Century, 1971
Barton, R. M., Life In Cornwall: In The Late 19th Century, 1972
Barton, R. M., Life In Cornwall: At The End of the 19th Century, 1974
Bates, Darrell, The Companion Guide to Devon & Cornwall, 1976
Betjeman, John, Cornwall, A Shell Guide, 1964
Burton, S. H., The West Country, 1972
Courtney, M. A., Cornish Feasts & Folklore, 1890
Davidson, Robin, Cornwalll, 1978
Deane, Tony & Shaw, Tony, The Folklore of Cornwall, 1975
Duncan, Ronald, Devon & Cornwall, 1966
Dyer, James, The Penguin Guide to Prehistoric England & Wales, 1981
Eagle, Dorothy & Carnell, Hilary, The Oxford Literary Guide To The British Isles, 1977
Evans, R. E., & Prettyman, G. W., Pentewan, 1986
Farr, Grahame, West Country Passenger Steamers, 1956
Folliott Stokes, A. G., From Land's End To The Lizard, 1909
Gibbons, Gavin, A Geographia Guide Cornwall & The Isles of Scilly
Greenhill, Basil, The Merchant Schooners, 1951
Hamilton Jenkin, A. K., Cornwall And Its People, 1945
Hammond, Reginald, J. W., & Lowther, Kenneth. E., Complete Cornwall, 1977
Hudson, Kenneth, The History Of English China Clays
Lambert, J. W., The Penguin Guides, Cornwall, 1939
Lane, John, Unknown Cornwall, 1925
MacDermot, E. T., History Of The Great Western Railway, Vol 2 (1863-1921)
Mee, Arthur, The King's England, Cornwall, 1937
Messenger, Michael, J., Caradon & Looe, The Canal, Railways & Mines, 1978
Noall, Cyril & Farr, Grahame: Wreck & Rescue Round The Cornish Coast
1: The Story of the North Coast Lifeboats, 1964
2: The Story of the Land's End Lifeboats, 1965
3: The Story of the South Coast Lifeboats, 1965
O'Toole, Laurence, The Roseland Between River & Sea, 1978
Payne, H. M. Cresswell, The Homeland Guide To The North Coast of Cornwall
Pevsner, Nikolaus, & Radcliffe, Enid, The Buildings of England, Cornwall, 1951
Roddis, Roland, Cornish Harbours, 1951
Salmon, Arthur, L., The Heart Of The West
Salmon, Arthur, L., The Little Guide, Cornwall, 1903
Turner, James, The Stone Peninsula, 1975
Ward, C. S., & Baddeley, M. J. B., Thorough Guide Series, South Devon & South Cornwall (1895)

Murray's Handbook Devon & Cornwall, 1865
The Travellers' Guides Cornwall & The Isles of Scilly, 1965
Ward Lock's Red Guide South Cornwall
Ward Lock's Red Guide North Cornwall
Ward Lock's Complete Cornwall
Ward Lock's Penzance & West Cornwall
Newspapers
The Falmouth Packet, The West Briton, The Royal Cornwall Gazette & Cornwall County News, The Cornishman & Cornish Telegraph, The Western Morning News.